LOVE

Mark Vernon

ALL THAT
MATTERS

ALL THAT
MATTERS

First published in Great Britain in 2013 by Hodder & Stoughton. An Hachette
UK company.
First published in US in 2013 by The McGraw-Hill Companies, Inc.
This edition published 2013
British Library Cataloguing in Publication Data: a catalogue record for this title is
available from the British Library.
Library of Congress Catalog Card Number: on file.
10 9 8 7 6 5 4 3 2 1
Typeset by Cenveo Publisher Services.
Printed in Great Britain by CPI Group (UK) Ltd, Croydon, CR0 4YY
Hodder & Stoughton policy is to use papers that are natural, renewable
and recyclable products and made from wood grown in sustainable forests.
The logging and manufacturing processes are expected to conform to the
environmental regulations of the country of origin.
Hodder & Stoughton Ltd
338 Euston Road
London NW1 3BH
www.hodder.co.uk

For my brother, Matthew

Contents

Introduction

Many stories have been told about love, exploring the way it works, the way it hurts, its delight and promise. This book tells the tale so as to bring together psychology and myth, ideas philosophers have had about love and experiences people have of love.

It is the story of love as love emerges across the course of a human life. The working thesis is that this happens in, broadly, three stages. At each stage a different capacity for love becomes possible, one deeper and more expansive than what was previously known. However, the transition between each mode is painful because it requires letting go of the security that comes with the former familiar love. A life will tend to go well, an individual will be more likely to flourish, if they can wisely utilize and spontaneously enjoy each kind of love. Conversely, things will tend to become stuck and troubled, perhaps seriously damaged, when a to-and-fro movement between the loves is blocked.

The three loves begin with self-love or, to give it its seemingly darker, more technical name, narcissism. In life, this is our first love, as the evidence is that it is the kind of love with which we are born. On the whole, it serves us well because it ensures we survive. It selfishly demands the nourishment and security, both physical and psychological, that the newborn child needs. However, there is a downside. Narcissism has little or no appreciation that other human beings exist as separate entities in the world. So, unless it is transcended, this love leaves us lonely and isolated, worried by the existence of others and untrusting. We must love ourselves but in such a way that we can get over ourselves and be comfortable in our own skin. Then narcissism serves us well because it means we can embrace a world apart from ourselves.

That leads to the second kind of love, the love that discovers there is another person in the world and this person is both loveable and returns love. Typically, it is thought that it begins to dawn on the very young child that it has a mother, or a primary carer, who is devoted to it. The infant is encouraged in play to explore the little intimacies that this other person longs to share and it develops the capacity for a healthy attachment to this other. The bodily warmth of their twosome nurtures in it the wonderful realization that it is not alone. The child grows in love, develops a stronger sense of itself through this relationship and, all being well, lays down capacities that will serve it well when, as a young adult, it falls in love and discovers once more that there is another person who might love them and whom they might love.

The second love supports a happy state of affairs, one that might be thought of as the pinnacle of love, particularly in its grown-up form – romantic love. But, in fact, it is a crucial part of the story told here that this is not the end of love. Left in that phase, romantic love is as limited and limiting as self-love. The two lovers are stranded, struggling to find fulfilment in each other, when, in truth, fulfilment for human beings requires far more than love focused on just one other person.

So the individual must make another transition, which again is difficult. However, if once more it navigates the shift well enough, a third even more tremendous experience of love comes into view. It is the love that can welcome a third dimension into its embrace. It is the most expansive and open, and with it the individual can throw him- or herself wholeheartedly into life.

The first experience of this third love is likely to occur when the now not quite so young child realizes Mother has other interests and loves, not least the individual she relates to as her beloved. That comes as a shock to the child, although he or she may then sense that Dad loves him or her as well as Mum, and that their threesome enables all kinds of experiences that were inconceivable before. One of the most astonishing is when the child notices it can observe two others loving, as he or she watches on, which leads to the sense that he or she too is being watched. Internalized, this is the basis for self-awareness and self-consciousness, and the sense that the centre of life is not focused on me, or between me and another, but is dispersed throughout fields or networks of shared loving connection.

Life is much more promising, and complex, and at times frightening, than the infant could have possibly imagined. With this third love, the child – and then adult – develops the confidence and trust required to enter into mature love and so to be a friend, pursue interests and passions, all in all to reach out into the life that it first tasted, though only in part, in the nursery.

▲ Jacques-Louis David, *Cupid and Psyche*, oil on canvas, 1817. The myth of Cupid and Psyche, physical and spiritual love, speaks of the unity of love, body and soul.

Again, this stage brings risks. Getting the hang of love is always tricky and on occasion it is perhaps thwarted. But on the whole, it is worthwhile because human beings are less than human when alone. The aim is that an individual has access to this repertoire of loves – self-love, love of another, and love of the unexpected that comes from life – and can deploy each flexibly and warmly when required.

This account of love's emergence in life is shaped by contemporary developmental psychology as well as the insights of psychotherapy. A lot of research has been gathered in the last two or three decades, focusing on aspects such as the way children attach to parents and the way parents attune to children. What is particularly exciting about this new work is that it chimes with older insights, too, not least those captured in the many myths and moral stories that explore the dynamics and dangers of love. The advantage that myths have is that they speak of real, if symbolic, characters. That brings an aliveness to the discussion because the characters speak directly to the anxieties and hopes of our inner lives. Examining the details of a good myth is to examine possibilities for ourselves; to heed warnings and to gain insights into ways forward. Myths are brilliant guides to love.

The book is in nine chapters. Chapter 1 focuses on self-love and narcissism. We next come, in Chapter 2, to the love a young child discovers with its primary carer, and then, in Chapter 3, we will think about romantic love as it is so connected to this earlier stage. (Think of all the words that we use for both our children and lovers: baby, darling, angel, dear one, precious, treasure.) Romantic love is one of the loves about which our culture is most confused, so it is worth unpicking.

We then come to a first interlude – Chapter 4 – to ask about the meaning of sex, before arriving at Chapter 5, which introduces the third love, the one that is three-dimensional. Its ups and downs are explored, not least in relation to human beings' amazing capacity for self-awareness. This self-awareness is so rich but also so painful that in Chapter 6 – our second interlude – we look at related difficulties from a different perspective.

In Chapter 7 we consider what I take to be the most wonderful human product of the third love, the capacity for friendship and, more generally, the sense of social and cultural belonging. Chapter 8 asks whether it is right to say that love is a feeling, as a third interlude. Then, in Chapter 9, we wonder just how expansive love can become and whether it might even open our eyes to transcendent dimensions of existence. A first appendix of 100 ideas offers ways of continuing the exploration of love while a second examines Plato's concept of love a little more deeply.

'The course of love never did run smooth', the proverb says. That is only because love is as fearsome and unexpected as the gift it offers to us, called life.

First love:
Narcissism

All that matters is love and work.

Sigmund Freud

ALL THAT
MATTERS

▶ His Majesty the Baby

Each of us was born a god. Or at least, as a newborn baby, we thought we were divine. Sigmund Freud had a phrase for it – he wrote of 'His Majesty the Baby'.

Our imagined omnipotence had to do with survival. We put ourselves first to maximize the chances of staying alive, and look what happened. You felt thirst and screamed? Sweet milk fell, as if by magic, on to your expectant tongue. You experienced discomfort and moaned? The wetness or chill disappeared. You wanted to sleep again and turned over? Warm sheets and blankets enfolded you. We assumed, as it were, upon arrival in life that life was there to serve us. It was, often, quite blissful. Such self-love is the first love of our lives.

Freud called this primary narcissism. It seems to be experienced as a kind of utopia, an environment that is entirely at the very young infant's beck and call. In the earliest days, psychologists debate the point but perhaps up to the age of about two months, studies suggest that infants have little sense that other individuals exist as separate whole individuals. The inference is, therefore, that they are fulfilling their needs themselves: they command and their wish occurs.

Self-love performed such miracles. The infant felt at one with the world and it was at one with the child. All was one. This is not so surprising as caring parents organize the nursery to be precisely adapted to their baby's desires, to be in sync with its demands and

▲ Helfrich Peter Sturz, *Princess Louise Augusta of Denmark as a Child*, pastel, 1771, Rosenborg Castle, Denmark. The Princess Louise Augusta was literally 'Her Majesty the Baby', though Freud's insight is that we all once thought of ourselves this way.

rhythms. Having no awareness of what it takes to organize the nursery, or even that there is a nursery, the whole of life seems to the infant to be for him or her, if not to *be* him or her. In a sense, it is. Human beings are born too young, a recent theory being that this is in order to allow our oversized heads to traverse the birth canal. As a result, we are not like dolphin pups that can swim alongside their mother immediately after birth. We are physically and psychologically defenceless. Even mammals like dogs or cats can be separated from their mothers after a few weeks. We do not just need months, but years. The young baby's dependency upon its primary carer is total.

Research carried out by psychologists and psychotherapists supports these conclusions. Observations of babies indicate that they are born primed to expect that the world will respond to them. After only 15 hours, they can distinguish their mother's voice and prefer it to that of strangers. It is similarly the case with the mother's smell and face. Other experiments demonstrate that the infant is calmed by hearing recordings of its own cry, and becomes upset at the crying of other babies. They like to hear the sound of their own and their mother's voice, presumably experienced as theirs too, and *only* those voices.

Evidence that neonates feel at one with the world is provided by watching how they respond to the changing expressions of their carers. At birth, children have nearly all the facial flexibility of an adult, though it takes them a few weeks to develop independent emotional expressions. Before then, they are very sensitive to the faces of parents. They will show surprise, fear, joy and interest in tandem with that of a carer. It is as if, for them, what is going on outside is the same as what is going on inside. Subject and object are one. There is no distinction.

The 'good-enough mother', as the paediatrician and psychoanalyst Donald Winnicott described her, colludes with this and is attuned to her offspring. He called it primary maternal preoccupation. She meets its physical needs and reflects its internal emotions. If she is good enough at doing so, she will help her child to sustain its illusion of narcissistic omnipotence. It is not just that food and blankets come as required; the whole environment echoes the feelings the child has, too. When it smiled, the world grinned back.

The idea of the command-and-control mentality of the very young child has been lent support by other ingenious research. In one experiment, an infant is trained in the delusion that it can turn music off and on. What happens is that when the infant is sucking, music turns off and on according to the rhythm of its sucking. The child soon comes to assume that it can turn the music off and on. Then, the experimenters turn the music off against the sucking pattern. The sound fails to 'obey' the child. The infant becomes distressed, crying and whimpering. His, or Her, Majesty has been defied.

Alternatively, behaviourists have looked to the words that the slightly older child typically comes to speak first. The paediatrician Arnold Gesell noted that possessive pronouns come first: 'mine' comes before 'me', which is in turn only then followed by 'you' and then 'I'. Parents may well recall the entertaining memory of their child referring to itself by its own name, in the third person: 'Sophie want crimbles!', 'More for Matthew!' It seems that the narcissistic desire to have stuff is so strong and necessary that it precedes the sense of having a self with which to possess it. That's the survival instinct.

Written in the body

Narcissism lodges itself very deep in the child. It is rooted in the body. Jean Piaget, one of the twentieth century's leading developmental psychologists, noticed how a child solved the problem of opening the lid of a box only when it opened its mouth. The movement prompted the idea of how to open the box. In other words, the body provides our first template for the world because we assume that our body and the world are intimately connected. The infant sucks in; forces out; draws near; pushes away; tests its strength; succumbs to its weakness; feels delight; trembles with dread; longs to hold as it is held; panics when it is falling because it feels like it might be falling apart. A primarily embodied way of engaging, understanding and manipulating the environment develops as a result.

The poet William Wordsworth described himself at this stage as holding 'mute dialogues with my Mother's heart' (*The Prelude*, Book II). His relationship with his mother was so seamless that it seemed to him he was inside her body. This is the adorable tyranny that the young child wreaks upon its parents. Its first sense of self was, ideally, to have no sense of being a separate self. That would have been too alarming, overwhelming. Its slightest reactions brought parents running, so that, as swiftly as possible, it could return to a state of calm, contented indifference. They loved you for it.

▶ An edgy love

That said, there is a price to pay. Your parents probably sensed that you were the most important creature in creation. They probably sent their friends your photo, remarking: Look at the most beautiful child in the world! But they were probably filled with anxieties, too. Mothers report dreams reflecting the enormity of the demand that their child makes upon them. In one reported case, a woman dreamed that she put her child in the car boot and then forgot it was there, only to remember, horrified, a couple of days later. Another dreamed that her child turned into a monster, attached to her like a leech, mercilessly sucking her milk and blood dry. Such is the rule of the gods. Little wonder mothers sing violent nursery rhymes to their offspring:

> *Hush-a-bye baby,*
>
> *On the tree top.*
>
> *When the wind blows,*
>
> *The cradle will rock.*
>
> *When the bough breaks,*
>
> *The cradle will fall.*
>
> *And down will come baby,*
>
> *Cradle and all.*

That is one way to relieve the tension of life with a young narcissist.

Hence, perhaps, the reason the word 'narcissism' carries ugly, disparaging connotations. My thesaurus lists 'vanity', 'conceit', 'self-importance' and 'self-absorption'. It is a shame in a way because primary narcissism is normal, healthy and good. Things go wrong psychologically for the young child when it does not feel the centre of attention. Without that comfort and protection, it can come to dwell in a perpetual state of fear and learn that life is a threat. It needs to love its body because its body is its first and basic tool for finding a way into and through the outside world.

An infant must know that it is loved because, only then, can it trust the risky business of coming to love others. Narcissism resources us as life unfolds, bringing confidence and courage, spontaneity and drive, a sense of safety and of being grounded. That must be why it is our first love.

And yet, it is also the case that primary narcissism must make way for different ways of engaging with the world. If it dominates for too long, then the capacity to love others as individuals who are separate and 'not-me' is hampered and restricted. Similarly, if the child's early and healthy narcissism is interfered with in some way – perhaps through abuse or a lack of care that blows holes in its self-esteem – then a number of profound difficulties can arise in adulthood, sometimes categorized as narcissistic personality disorders.

The dangers of narcissism are captured in the myth from which we derive the word itself, the ancient story of Echo and Narcissus. It goes like this.

▶ The myth of Narcissus

Narcissus was the son of the river god Cephissus and the nymph Liriope, who gave birth to him after Cephissus enveloped Liriope in his waters. Right from

Pathological narcissist disturbance

Psychologists have identified at least three types of adult narcissism that are not healthy but may lead to mental ill-health. Individuals suffering from each type are known as the empowered narcissist, the manipulative narcissist and the impoverished narcissist:

1 The empowered narcissist is successful, frequently charismatic and often singled out as a leader. They enjoy the esteem that comes with power, though their difficulties with love are marked by sadder, ruthless and grandiose aspects. Closer observation still reveals that they work hard at maintaining admiring, needy audiences and are disabled when it comes to forming intimate interpersonal relationships.

2 The manipulative narcissist is a great reader of other people's minds, a talent that they use to charm and seduce. Their goal is to make sure that they have loyal and admiring people around them. They could be said to feed off others because they have little capacity to sustain love themselves. Seen close up, these individuals appear fragile and thin-skinned, arising from a precarious sense of self.

3 The disempowered narcissist is never satisfied with him- or herself. They may pass examinations, have good jobs, and may be married with a family, but it never feels enough. Their low-esteem is often evident. It is not hidden behind carapaces of brilliance like the other types of narcissism. They may be passive in relationships or come across as withdrawn or aloof. Sometimes they admit that they feel empty inside or that life seems pointless.

ALL THAT MATTERS: LOVE

▶ Adult narcissism

Everyone is narcissistic to a degree. Possessing narcissistic aspects to your personality does not mean that you have a narcissistic personality disorder. It was your first love. It is lodged deep inside. The question is whether, as an adult, self-love enables the individual to flourish as he or she is supposed to or whether it is destructive of their humanity because it prevents them from loving others. The story of Narcissus relates what happens when someone is not able to love him- or herself appropriately. Conversely, the person who is able to love him- or herself appropriately is able to get over him- or herself. They do not need perpetually to gaze into the mirror or talk about themselves. They have neither an over-inflated sense of themselves, nor do they constantly put themselves down – the self-hate that is really narcissism in reverse. They can turn away from the pool and understand that there is a world around them to love. This can happen only when a good experience of being loved as a child is firmly embedded within them. They have confidence that they are lovely enough. This allows them to have intimacy with others.

Psychotherapists call it possessing ego strength. Psychologists talk of self-esteem or positive self-image. More colloquially, it is about being comfortable in your own skin, being at ease with yourself. Such people are a delight to be with because they have time for others. They do not constantly draw attention to themselves. They have love to give because they have been offered love before and were able to receive it.

It is, therefore, worth asking why narcissism carries such automatically negative associations. In our culture, selfishness has become a loaded quality to be avoided at all costs. It may have something to do with religious injunctions around the notion that it is better to give than to receive, though I suspect the difficulty is more recent than this blaming of religion implies. The word 'altruism', for example, is only a century or so old. It was invented by the nineteenth-century sociologist Auguste Comte. It was as if he felt the need to distinguish the good love of selflessness from the supposed bad love of selfishness and drive a binary opposition between them.

Narcissism is problematic in our times, as the psychologist Thomas Moore agrees. In his book *Care of the Soul*, he argues that a lack of subtlety around the subject of self-love, and the frequency with which problems to do with self-esteem and self-image appear in the consulting room, speaks of a trivialized sense of what it is to be human. He writes:

> [M]any people seem to have difficulty distinguishing narcissism from a proper and necessary love of self. Therefore, the person confused about being too hungry for praise holds back from the pleasure of achievement. He makes little of an obvious success or has difficulty accepting compliments and praise, thinking that in this way he will avoid the dreaded narcissism. False humility denies the ego the attention it craves, but the denial itself is narcissistic, since it is a negative focus on ego rather than on the pleasurable possibilities of life.

Thomas Moore, *Care of the Soul* (London: HarperCollins, 1992), p. 72

It is as if our understanding of ourselves has become too individualistic, too mechanical. The developmental sense of love has been lost and so self-love is not understood as a phase we go through, building one modality of love, which allows us to love others. 'No man is an island' is an oft-heard refrain, though it sounds rather desperate because our culture does in fact implicitly regard people as isolated individuals. We worry about autonomy more than connection, about freedom over commitment. It is as if the default image that the Western mind has of itself is the billiard ball. We jostle and bounce off each other for fear of touching and holding one another. Could the wariness of narcissism be because our culture is secretly, unhealthily, narcissistic?

Moore's key insight is that the kind of self-love that enables human beings to flourish cannot be demanded or forced. It must be given to us, like the mother who gives her child the capacity to love others by loving her child herself. If being loveable is viewed as a possession or performance, and so a question of fashion or display, then that puts a block on receiving and discovering love through receiving and discovering the love of another person. The quest for the perfect body repeats Narcissus' fate in that it is absorbed with the image on the surface. It is caught at the level of the ephemeral and becomes stuck in the shallows. Such an individual cannot see the depths of another's soul because they have never gazed into the depths of their own being. Moore continues:

The narronisstic person simply does not know how profound and interesting his nature is. In his narcissism he is condemned to carry the weight of life's responsibilities on his own shoulders... Narcissism may look like an indulgent pleasure, but beneath the façade of satisfaction lies an oppressive burden. The narcissistic person tries very hard to be loved, but he never succeeds because he doesn't realize yet that he has to love himself as other before he himself can be loved.

Thomas Moore, *Care of the Soul*
(London: HarperCollins, 1992), p. 72

We can summarize the perils of narcissism as follows:

The troubled narcissist is good at:	The healthy individual is good at:
Self-preservation	Hearing others
Possessing	Receiving
Image	Depth
Singleness of mind	Changing views
Clarity	Paradox
Controlling	Letting go
Holding fast	Reflecting
Having sex	Making love

The story of Narcissus appears to end badly. The beautiful young man realizes that the image is only a reflection of himself and simultaneously realizes that he cannot break the habit. He is made that way, and the only way out is to die.

But the appearance of the flower is a token of hope. The hard pride of the youth gives way to the soft delicacy of the yellow bloom. What the myth suggests is that narcissism is not the sum total of our engagement with the world. Instead, it can sink into the ground of our being and feed us like the soil does the flower. This is what happens when the very young infant has a good-enough parent. Primary narcissism equips us well and a new love becomes possible, the love of another. It is to that second love we now turn.

2

It takes two

Love is the extremely difficult realization that something other than oneself is real.

Iris Murdoch

▶ Love is painful

Whenever love is written about, pain is never far away. Love seems umbilically linked to loss, to longing, to hurting. Then, there are the religious portrayals of love. In Christianity, divine love is conveyed by a man dying on a cross. 'Greater love hath no man...' the biblical quote goes (John 15:13). It is even said that love will kill the thing that it loves. In his poem *The Ballad of Reading Gaol*, Oscar Wilde lamented how love's murderous intent is variously enacted – with a look, a word, a kiss, a sword.

Love is said to conquer fear, too, to forgive, and to bring an end to suffering. But why is it that love seems required to undergo painful rites of deep distress, or to put it another way: why is love so risky?

One way to answer that question follows from the reflections on narcissism of the last chapter. Narcissism is the love of one, the love of oneself to be precise. It is a necessary love, though a self-limiting – self-limited – love. It must find a place within us in order that we learn to trust life. And then its ruthlessness must be overcome, so that its protective shell does not leave us isolated and falling into the black hole of a solipsistic universe.

This expansive task, breaking free of the confines of the self, is the source of the pain. The love of one is fragile because the narcissist believes he or she is self-sufficient. It is a delusion, though a comforting one: I need not depend on others, with all the wayward unreliability they might bring. And yet, opening up to others, learning to bear the cares and concerns of loving others, must happen if the individual is to grow. Human beings are not one, in fact, and the first step towards understanding that is learning to become part of two.

Friedrich Nietzsche, the German philosopher who knew a thing or two about the pain of isolation, argued that human beings can be a bit like the castle pieces in a chess set. Much of our lives is spent running up and down the stone staircase inside these solitary turrets. Sometimes we reach the top and glimpse blue sky over the battlements. Often we fall to the bottom and find ourselves groping around in the darkness of our own grey dungeons. And every so often, we pass by a slit window. If we stop for a moment, we realize that it is an opening through our thick walls. If we glance out, we see other castles near us. We see other self-contained individuals also robustly defended against the threats of the world. And we might ask ourselves: can we reach out?

▶ There is another

It is an early, primitive question, one faced by the young infant. Psychologists debate how long primary narcissism dominates the neonate's emotional landscape. Perhaps it is a month, maybe three. Whatever the actual answer, a shift occurs when His Majesty the Baby realizes that he or she is not a god after all.

It is a shock. The not-quite-so-young child begins to notice that its desires are not fulfilled in all haste. It wanted sustenance that did not promptly come. It sought warmth and was left cold, for a while. There is a gap. Sometimes something else happens. An alien force interrupts it. The child finds that its thumb is pulled from its mouth. It is awoken from sleep, lifted and disturbed. Its dignity and power is offended.

The reaction is violent. Many children will scream, struggle and yell. There may be a touch of panic in its voice, perhaps as it senses its impotence. Then, a kind of primitive game of revenge may ensue. When the nipple is offered, it is rejected even though the child feels hungry. When the sheets return to enfold, the warmth is refused as little legs kick them off.

One can speculate that this very refusal causes a new possibility to dawn at the edges of a still-immature mind. Are there forces in this world that are beyond my control? Is there a presence, let us call her 'Mother', who is the truly powerful one? Do others really exist? Like Adam and Eve in the mythical garden, the nursery that the child had implicitly assumed was made for it, and it alone, begins to evoke troubling feelings of nakedness and unease.

It is a process that must be negotiated successfully. For some children, it is relatively easy. For others, it is not. Much may depend upon how the child's primary carers themselves coped with *their* early narcissistic feelings. But, without the wrenches and pain, the child will not only not be able to love others well; it will not be able to know itself fully as a self, with physical boundaries and emotional limitations, tested by the experience of rubbing up against others. The self is found only in relationship.

I wonder whether this is the meaning of the story of Alice going through the looking glass, the looking glass being a metaphor for the solipsistic phase in which the world is taken to be a reflection of yourself. As that delusion dies – as Alice goes through the looking glass – she begins to see that everything she thought was familiar is actually strange. Poetry must be read backwards. The chess pieces come to life. The White Queen remembers future events as if they were

▲ Illustration by John Tenniel from *Alice's Adventures in Wonderland* (1865) by Lewis Carroll.

in the past. The world appears as a place of nonsense. Nothing is quite what it seems.

This upsets Alice. But it is a distressing rite she must undergo. Like the young child who kicks and screams, she wakes up to the life of others by violently shaking the Red Queen. It is as if she is exorcising the monarchical tyrant who was herself, the Red Queen as Her Majesty the Baby.

On the whole, the distress is worth it. A more accurate sense of reality is disorienting at first, and then, gradually, a richer world is perceived, one containing depths that narcissism could never imagine. At the heart of it is the love of another: the young child realizes it has a mother.

'Mother' stands here for primary carer. The evidence is that it need not be the biological and female parent who offers the child this love. What seems important is that the infant can relate and attach to one person who has their interests at heart and who is prepared and able to sacrifice their own interests to care for it. Winnicott called this the 'ordinary devotion' of a mother, a phrase that nicely combines the deep love and commitment that raising a child demands with the everyday nature of the task. It is replicated in countless millions of households across the planet.

Ordinary devotion is not only exemplified in the business of feeding the child and keeping it warm; it is a psychological task, too. This is where love in the emotional sense is vital. The primary carer must be able reliably to engage with the child's inner life, particularly its anxieties. That empathic awareness helps the infant to process its fears so that it does not disappear into

▲ Hodegetria icon from the church of the Physician Saints the Greater, Ohrid, Macedonia, tempera on wood, thirteenth century. The image of the Madonna and Child – Mary and Jesus – conveys something of the ideal intimacy between mother and child, together and yet separate.

itself, and develop desperate habits of trying to hold itself together: it learns to trust and depend upon another to help it through the challenges of the day. It is a vital achievement if mature love is to be possible later on. Further, the primary carer communicates an enjoyment of life through his or her enjoyment of the child. The way the young infant is handled, kissed, held and nurtured speaks of the pleasure of being loved. The look of a loving eye, the sound of a soft voice, holds the child as much as the caring arm. This expression of love welcomes young life into life.

▶ Love as attunement

It has been called 'attunement' by the behavioural psychologist Daniel Stern. Attunement is the ability of the primary carer to share in the inner life of the child so that the child develops a growing sense of its own inner life and the inner lives of others. It is a kind of psychic intimacy that leaves us with a new feel for the world, one that can sense, desire and engage the presence of others. The young child is left with what Stern calls a 'core' sense of itself, a solidity and reliance felt in the body, and also a 'subjective' sense of itself, one that now knows itself in relation to others.

Gradually, the baby learns that it is held in mind by another. Though risky, because it relies on another, this love brings a much deeper sense of security than narcissism alone can supply. The world can be experienced in a grounded way, a friendly as well as a fearful place. Winnicott provides a humdrum example of the difference it makes, one that almost every parent will appreciate. 'Think of an infant expecting a feed,' he writes in his paper 'From dependence towards independence', '...the time comes when the infant can wait a few minutes because noises in the kitchen indicate that food is about to appear. Instead of simply being excited by the noises, the infant uses the news item in order to be able to wait.' When a child can wait for a few minutes that is because it knows there are others upon whom it can rely. The task of parenting is massively relieved.

When attunement goes wrong

Stern discusses how maternal attunement can go wrong. There may be misattunement – that is, routine and persistent under-reactions to the child on the part of the primary carer. It leads to a sense of being distant and isolated from life, as if not truly alive. A second problem is inauthentic attunement, when the parent's heart is not in it. This is inevitable from time to time, but, again, if the parent is routinely psychically absent, depressed or too tired, it will undo the love a parent and child should enjoy.

Stern also discusses the opposite, over-attunement, when the primary carer seeks 'to crawl' inside the child's experience – to live their own life through that of their child. In time, this can destroy the infant's sense of its own agency by undermining the sense that it is distinct from the parent. It will gain little clear sense of itself.

Being able to wait for food or for another is an ability born of the second kind of love. Conversely, the individual – adult or child – who is unable to wait conveys the agonizing secret that they do not trust the world and do not feel loved. The impatience speaks of the unbearable suspicion that the world will let you down because kindness, care and intimacy do not underwrite life. The fear is that the brute fact of existence is the opposite of love – indifference.

▶ Love as attachment

Another way of thinking about these misfirings of love is via attachment theory. According to the psychotherapist John Bowlby and others, only the child who has a good attachment with its carer will be able to step into the world with confidence and ease. Children who do not share in the reliable, secure love of a carer will develop a variety of distressing attachment styles. It is as if they learn uneasy or dysfunctional patterns for loving others at a young age that are replicated in the relationships they try to form in later life.

As an adult, some may become **ambivalently attached.** This can show itself later in clingy relationships, in which a lover is not really trusted; or in submissive relationships, in which love is implicitly interpreted as the requirement to acquiesce to the demands of a manipulative other. Love is experienced as tyrannical.

A second style is **avoidant attachment.** Adult relationships that are unconsciously deploying this model will convey an air of cool detachment, as if the relationship does not really matter, though in fact it does terribly. An avoidantly attached lover may, therefore, project a sense of relaxed and confident distance and yet, at the same time, be highly sensitive to the slightest perceived rebuff. Love is experienced as fragile.

A third style is known as **insecure disorganized.** It is the most painful of them all, leading to adult relationships that may warrant a pathological description. Love here is known as a hostile force characterized by the possibly violent need to control. The profound sadness of the situation comes across in the inability of the suffering individual, say, to hold another's gaze. The warm, romantic image of lovers staring into each other's eyes is experienced by this attachment style as a threat and an unbearable attack. Couples who come together because they share this disturbance are likely to share a mutually abusive relationship. They may injure one another in perverse enactments of their affections or perhaps seek love in joint and dangerous activities such as taking drugs.

That said, with good-enough loving, the child survives the transition from one to two. Thankfully, it often happens.

The psychotherapist Priscilla Roth calls this shift 'a developmental step of enormous proportions'. She continues:

> Loving [mother], when [the child] takes in her milk and the attention in her eyes and the comfort of her arms, he feels he has her in himself, he feels

loved and living inside himself. These are powerful and wonderful feelings. They are the feelings we search for and, if we are fortunate, find again later in adult form: a belief that we are loving and that we are loved.

Priscilla Roth, 'The depressive position', in S. Budd and R. Rusbridger (eds), *Introducing Psychoanalysis* (Routledge: Hove, 2005), p. 52

The child has moved from a life alone to the possibilities of life enabled by the capacity to love another.

Myths of romance

To be the perfect spouse would ruin any marriage.

Simon May

▶ Falling in love

Today, when people think of love, it is probably the romantic love of two that is imagined. The passionate adoring of starry-eyed lovers has gained a virtual monopoly on the collective fantasy conjured by the word 'love'. It is the adult version of the early mode of love first found with another, probably the mother. Falling in love is, in powerful ways, to repeat the experience, enjoying again the attention of another, the comfort of their arms, the feeling of being inside someone else. The way we first attuned to love will have an effect on the way we are now able to attune to a lover. The attachment style that first formed in us will play a part in the kind of relationship we find ourselves in as adults. So let us think about this love, too.

It is the love that overwhelms. It is imagined as stealing up on us unawares, gripping us like a creeper. It is experienced as magical or bewitching. Some are desperate for its promise. Others shun its sentimentality, perhaps sensing the partial return to infancy that wells up when people fall in love. It is an important insight, for, while romance is powerful and wonderful, and no one can resist it when it happens, it is not the end point of love, any more than our first parental pairing was the end of love then.

▶ Genes and brains

The natural sciences have turned an eye on romance and arrived at a range of theories. One branch draws on evolutionary biology. It asks how human beings have evolved the capacity for romance through Darwinian processes of natural selection. It must have adaptive advantage, the logic goes, which means that the genes of those who fall in love have a better chance of surviving. So what does the phenomenon of romance bring, for it is clearly not necessary to fall in love to have children? Perhaps a man is powerfully drawn to the curvaceous body of his beloved because her hips and breasts whisper of fecundity or good childrearing capacities. Perhaps a woman fantasizes about the taut stomach and thrusting musculature of that man because it promises potent seed. In other words, the reason the experience is so powerful is because we are being tricked. We are not falling in love as the romantic novelist describes it. Rather, our biology is just seeking the best available mate.

It is possible to object to this reading of romance by noting that falling in love is a wildly inefficient process simply to ensure the perpetuation of genes. It exhausts a considerable amount of excess energy. Further, when people fall in love, they tend to neglect and forget themselves. That may not matter much these days, but on the savannah, when wild beasts lurked behind every shrub and stalked our ancestors as prey, not caring about anything but love might have had a considerable survival disadvantage. 'Love is blind' is one of the oldest sayings on the subject. Blindness is lethal in the jungle.

The evolutionary explanation has a riposte to that. It notes that raising children is a costly affair. For women, bearing children has long been intimately associated with death – in childbirth. For men, feeding and defending children is similarly risky, far harder than simply looking after yourself. Romance evolved, it is said, to ensure that intelligent primates such as ourselves will discount the risks and commit to the long and dangerous task of the survival of the next generation.

However, other evolutionary biologists object again, pointing out that this line of thought turns love into a cost–benefit analysis. It is as if we no longer needed the poets to tell us about love because accountants can do a better job. Love clearly has a biological component but it also clearly has dimensions that transcend the demands of survival. The need to propagate might actually be hitching a ride on the desire to love, rather than the other way round. (See the interlude 'What is sex for?' in the following chapter.)

A parallel critique can be levelled at a second branch of the contemporary science of love. It looks not to evolution to explain romance, but to the brain. Consider the work of Andreas Bartels and Semir Zeki, published in a paper entitled 'The neural basis of romantic love'. They had a series of subjects look at pictures of their beloved, and then pictures of their friends, while they were lying in a brain scanner. The scientists then subtracted the areas of the brain that were active when viewing the friends from the areas of the brain that were active when gazing on their lovers. The remainder, 'a limited expanse of the cortex', was called the 'love spot'.

An incisive rebuttal of this work has been offered by another neuroscientist, Raymond Tallis, who also has the advantage of being a philosopher. In *Aping Mankind:*

Neuromania, Darwinitis and the Misrepresentation of Humanity, he highlights various technical problems with the science, such as how brain scanners average results and so lose details. But his main complaint is that the methodology cannot grasp the richness of the experiential nature of love. He writes:

> [L]ove is not like a response to a simple stimulus such as a picture. It is not even a single enduring state, like being cold. It encompasses many things, including: not feeling in love at that moment; hunger; indifference; delight; wanting to be kind; wanting to impress; worrying over the logistics of meetings; lust; awe; surprise; joy; guilt; anger; jealousy; imagining conversations or events; speculating what the loved one is doing when one is not there; and so on.

> Raymond Tallis, *Aping Mankind*
> (Acumen: Durham, 2011), p. 77

All in all, Tallis concludes, 'The neuro-evolutionary pseudo-sciences tend to base their ... conclusions on experiments that grotesquely simplify human life.' So how else, then, might we explore this enormously complex and entirely commonplace experience?

Psychology, I think, offers a better way forward, particularly around the core insight that when we fall in love we revisit our earliest experience of love. There is evidence to support the theory, in that we develop attachment styles in the early months of life that, to a degree, shape our subsequent romantic relationships.

This needs to be nuanced, of course. It is perhaps better to say that the love of our more mature years is in dialogue with the love learned in infancy – not determined by it, but working through it in one way or another.

So how can we take this agenda on? Well, much as myth came to our aid when thinking about narcissism, so myth can take us into the dynamics of romance, too, as well as offering guidance and warnings. Love has generated countless such moral stories. But there is one that has influenced the way we talk about it, probably more than any other.

▶ Aristophanes' story

In the *Symposium*, a dialogue about love written around 385 BC, Plato puts a myth about romance into the mouth of the ancient Greek comic writer Aristophanes. It is a fantastic tale that has captured the Western imagination ever since.

Long ago, Plato has Aristophanes begin, our nature was not as it is now, but was very different. There were three kinds of human beings: males and females, and also hermaphrodites, an androgynous combination of male and female. They were all completely round, having four hands, legs and ears, and two faces and sets of genitals. They moved by spinning with great rapidity, like gymnasts doing cartwheels.

This mode of locomotion lent them strength, and bred in our ancestors an insatiable desire for power.

The ambition alarmed the gods, who feared human beings might make an assault on them. The king of the gods, Zeus, was perplexed about what to do. He could not destroy the human race with thunderbolts, Aristophanes says, because then there would be no one to offer the gods sacrifices and libations. And where would gods be without that?

Then, Zeus had an idea. He cut each human in two. This way, people lost their strength but increased in number, thereby halving the threat and doubling the worship. Human navels, Aristophanes ventures – again, tongue firmly in cheek – are where Apollo sewed up the wound caused by the severance. But then things started to go awry.

The humans longed for their other half. They became like flatfish, seeking a match that looked like the lost slice. Poor souls, they would limp across the face of the Earth throwing their arms around each other, hoping to embrace their lost partner. They came to believe that the only way their lives could be complete was by falling in love. And it had to be the right person, the individual who would return them to the physical and spiritual union of their aboriginal state. This made love perilous, for there was every chance that you might not find the perfect match. The world is a big place. If you hold the belief that there is one person out there for you, there is paradoxically less and not more chance of finding happiness in love. Aristophanes says that depressed humans started to neglect themselves. They fell hungry and became idle. Some despaired and died.

Zeus then had another plan. He moved the genitals of the men and women around so that when they met they could form a sexual union. This congress, even if it was not with the lost half, still delivered great pleasure. The men and women were at least partially satisfied, and when having sex they often felt life was complete. Moreover, having made love, the humans also returned to the important business of offering sacrifices and libations to the gods – until, that is, the need to make love stole up on them again.

The myth is a powerful way of conveying the notion that there is a unique, irreplaceable human being who must be found at all costs, regardless of the pain, for only then can life feel full. The story captures the experience and fits well with developmental psychology, which speaks, too, of a lost other – not a lover but a mother. 'This, then, is the source of our desire to love each other,' Aristophanes proposes. 'Love is born into every human being; it calls back the halves of our original nature together; it tries to make one out of two and heal the wound of human nature.'

There is a final twist to the story. When lovers meet, Hephaestus, the god of blacksmiths, passes by and asks the pair a question: What are they seeking? Perhaps to be welded together for ever? The lovers, of course, reply most affirmatively. What could seal their happiness more completely than melding together? They would then be happy to die together.

It is a dark twist. It raises the possibility that romantic love might, actually, be a form of delusion, enslavement. Give your life to the intensity of the romantic quest, and life might, literally, become a bind. Perhaps romance is a myth in the pejorative sense, a fabrication that we tell ourselves, that grips our souls – and lessens our lives. It would, indeed, be a return to an infantile stage, not so much a search for a presumed lost half as a search for the innocence of early love. Left at that, love will not carry us forward into life. It would leave us stuck somewhere in mode two.

Romance and authenticity

The ideal of romantic love can be traced back to Aristophanes' myth, but it has been argued that the seed sowed by Plato came to fruition only recently, in the eighteenth century. The philosopher Simon May argues that it was then that ideas about love focused on the hope that love authenticates the human soul. 'In love he becomes not selfless but a self,' May writes in his book *Love: A History*. 'He doesn't lose himself but finds himself.'

The key player in this transformation is the Swiss philosopher Jean-Jacques Rousseau. In his memoir *Les Rêveries du promeneur solitaire* (Reveries of the Solitary Walker), he recalls the time he fell in love as a young man, writing: 'I recall with joy and tenderness this unique and brief time of my life when I was myself, fully, without admixture and without obstacle, and when I can genuinely say that I lived.'

Under this philosophical dispensation, romance becomes its own end. It is a journey into passionate feeling that does not point beyond itself, but instead seeks a heightened sense of what it is to be human in that feeling. It is the love kick that counts. May calls this modern romantic sensibility the moment when 'love comes to fall in love with itself'. In marked contrast with Aristophanes' myth, it does not really matter whom you fall in love with, so long as sometime, some place, you fall in love.

▌ Beyond romance

The genius of Plato's story is that it is both an existential celebration and moral warning. Lovers do talk about looking for their other half. Others – perhaps having been in love – warn that love makes you greedy, jealous, angry, duplicitous, tired. All these themes are embedded in the original myth. Reflect upon its details and you reflect upon the experience of this kind of love.

The Latin name for the god of love, Cupid, also gives us the word 'cupidity', echoing the insatiable possessiveness of romantic love. Potentially, it longs for the beloved with such intensity that it might destroy the beloved in the process. Like Aristophanes' lovers, who are bound together by Hephaestus, romantic love of itself would have us not be ourselves but become lost in the one we love the most. This is the warning: romance is natural, unavoidable, good. But, like narcissism, it also has its limits.

It is not that we don't need or shouldn't want it. It sets the young person, fizzing with the possibilities of puberty, on a course that, ideally, leads to a mature relationship, one in which they can flourish for the rest of their lives. The point is that romance is a catalyst for union; it powers the search for another person. But, if the myth and the psychology is right, it should not itself be the end of that search. It needs to be saved from itself, lest it undo the lovers. Here, another myth might come to our aid. It suggests a way through romance to a further kind of love, one that expands love's possibilities beyond love shared only between two.

It also comes from ancient Athens and relates to a problem experienced by the infant god of love, Eros. The story goes that, as his first months passed by, the young child did not grow. He stayed the size he was at birth. He was somehow stuck in infancy, which was odd because he was otherwise full of life and energy. He wouldn't grow up.

His mother, Aphrodite, became perplexed and then distressed. She contacted her sister, the wise Themis, and begged for advice. 'Have a second son,' Themis counselled, 'and this time ensure that the father is Ares, the god of war. Call the child Anteros [meaning "equal of Eros"].' The siblings, she promised, would rival one another – joshing, scrapping, and then become reconciled. As Themis put it: 'These two brothers will be of the same nature, and each will be the cause of the other's growth; for as they see each other they will alike grow, but if either is left alone they will both waste away.'

Themis' plan worked. As long as the boys played and fought at one another's side, Eros grew up. His wings enlarged. His chubby flesh turned into resilient muscle. He matured. 'He needs his brother always besides him,' wrote the philosopher Themistius, who records the myth in his *Orations* ('An exhortation to the Nicomedians'). 'Sensing him large, he strives to prove himself greater, or finding him small and slight he often wastes unwillingly away.'

So what is the myth trying to say? The story of Eros and Anteros, and the rivalry between these two closely related loves, is not nearly as well known as that of

▲ The famous statue of *Eros* in Piccadilly Circus, London, has been argued by some to actually be of his brother, Anteros. Statue by Alfred Gilbert, aluminium, 1893.

Aristophanes. Little is remembered, either, about what the ancient Greeks made of it. What remains has been gathered together by Craig Stephenson, in his book *Anteros: A Forgotten Myth*. He notes that Pausanias, the great travel writer of the ancient world, describes an altar to Anteros beneath the Acropolis. It commemorates the death of Timagoras, a man who was madly in love with Meles. Timagoras proved his love by throwing himself to his death, at Meles' childish command, from the highest point of the rocky outcrop. It is another tale of the destructive power of this love when it becomes stuck. Meles, in turn, was ruined by the pangs of remorse that followed his silly demand. Immature love brought them both down. It is as if the two were possessed by a romantic daemon and, like the infant Eros, were unable to grow up.

By erecting an altar to Anteros on the spot where Timagoras died, it looks as if the Athenians were hoping that Anteros might inject a certain realism or discernment into the otherwise wild impulses of romantic love. Remember what can happen, it says to all lovers. Eros is the god who pierces lovers with his arrows, turning folk mad with desire. Surges of feeling, desperate experiences of longing, overtake and control the romantic lover's life if romance is his or her sole ruler. This second myth might be conveying that, if love is to flourish, romance needs to be counterbalanced, even opposed, by another force: Anteros. He might direct the passion towards mature love, much as the mother had to direct her child into a wider world.

Happy ever after

A modern retelling of the ancient myth of Anteros is found in Tolstoy's short story, 'Happy Ever After'. Masha falls in love with Sergey, though, after the first thrill of meeting, she finds herself tyrannized by romantic longings that she now fears will not be fulfilled. It is an agony all the more paradoxical because all that she had wanted from life was to be in love. She reflects:

> All that I had hardly dared to hope for had come to pass. My vague confused dreams had become a reality, and the reality had become an oppressive, difficult, and joyless life. All remained the same — the garden visible through the window, the grass, the path, the very same bench, the same song of the nightingale by the pond, the same lilacs in full bloom, the same moon shining above the house; and yet, in everything such a terrible inconceivable change! Such coldness in all that might have been near and dear!

> Leo Tolstoy, 'Happy Ever After', *The Kreutzer Sonata and Other Stories* (Oxford University Press: Oxford)

Luckily for Masha, the anterotic element is never lost in her passion for Sergey. It is expressed in the fact that they talk together. They talk together a lot. In that talking, she gradually redescribes her story. The dictatorship of idealized romance is not so much overthrown, which would hardly work because passion thrives on the tumult. Instead, it gradually dissolves.

Sergey calls it 'the nonsense of life'. When exposed, life can 'get back to itself'. As Tolstoy's story comes to an end, Masha recalls: 'I looked at him, and suddenly my heart grew light; it seemed that the cause of my suffering had been removed like an aching nerve.'

The myth points to what Anteros brings. Themis was a goddess known for being able to bring opposing energies together in the service of healing. There is passion but it is shaped by reason – the sensual coupled with common sense. As the early sixteenth-century proverb has it, 'The quarrel of lovers is the renewal of love.' The sibling rivalry of Eros and Anteros stands for a necessary discomfort and grit that pricks romance's bubble.

The myth is also clear that Anteros had to remain at the side of Eros in order that young love might continue to grow to maturity. When Anteros departed, Eros regressed to the chubby and babyish stage again. In other words, love needs a commitment to work through the ups and downs. It will not be easy. It takes practice. The myth is saying that love is tricky, perhaps requiring the effort of a lifetime to secure. A degree of rivalry between lovers – the rows and tense moments – is actually helpful. It is when romance is thought of as a fantasy – that life is perfected in love – that lovers should worry. The life-giving tension is captured in the iconography of Eros and Anteros who are typically depicted as wrestling, often over a symbolic item such as a palm branch, the sign of victory.

Striving is part and parcel of mature loving, the myth explains, as rivalry is part and parcel of having siblings. That may sound unsettling, disappointing or exhausting. Most people know couples who do nothing but argue, and with whom it is hard to be. But Anteros does not bring outright war to a relationship. His father was Ares, not he himself. Instead, mingled with the love of Aphrodite, he ultimately nurtures not combat but collaboration.

Dissimilarities are not watered down, for all that romantic lovers hate to be reminded of their differences. Rather, they are seen as wellsprings of growth, via love's exchange. If Eros is the great unifying force in the human psyche, Anteros compensates by ensuring that unity does not descend into dull uniformity. There is a distance as well as a closeness.

Put that alongside Aristophanes' myth and there would be a very different outcome when Hephaestus passes by. Lovers inspired by Anteros will resist his charming offer of melding. They will sense that an erotic tangle is not in their best interests. As the French philosopher Alain Badiou puts it: 'Everybody says love is about finding the person who is right for me and then everything will be fine. But it's not like that. It involves work. An old man tells you this!' Badiou is referring to himself, in a book entitled *In Praise of Love*. He explores how solving the problems of romantic love is 'one of life's great joys'. Anteros is god of these problems. They are sometimes trivial, such as working out who sleeps on which side of the bed. They may sometimes seem insuperable, such as deciding on the question of children. They can be tricky, such as negotiating whether this is a chaste relationship or one with room for lovers on the side. But in all cases, problems are life-giving when not avoided because they offer a reality check against which to put romantic fantasies to the test.

The principle is implicit in couples counselling. It may come as a surprise to those who first seek professional help with their relationships to learn that the therapist is not much interested in the harmonious parts of their life together, but the conflicts. A capacity not to shy away from them is essential for long-lasting love. Conversely, a fear of conflict is one predictor of divorce. The happy couple are often the pair who can embrace the rows and problems, perhaps almost welcome them, not because they like a fight but because they do not want tensions to mount. These lovers are able openly to explore the darker terrain in their relationship. They are not overly frightened by the shadows. Neither do they live by the hope that all is sunshine and light.

It is this dynamic element that the lovers in Aristophanes' myth don't get. Believing they have found their long-lost half, they are only too delighted to be joined permanently together. Only now, there is no distance between them. They are not two individuals together, but one creature who appears less than human. They slide to the ground and cling to one another. Believing their struggle is over, not only just begun, it is as if their life is over too.

▶ Erotic friendship

Plato knew of Anteros as well and includes him in another of his dialogues, the *Phaedrus*. This exchange between Socrates and a young man called Phaedrus contains more descriptions of the madness of love, portrayed in vivid terms: how lovers rush at one another like charging horses in the need to embrace. Such is the force that, to passers-by, it can be hard to tell whether the two are making love or engaged in some form of mutual rape. Bodies slam and lock together.

There is, though, a different quality of love that may emerge, Plato continues. When inspired by Anteros, the lovers perceive that their affection is not only sexual. It also contains the seeds of friendship, and deep friendship at that. 'Now that he allows his lover to talk and spend time with him, and the man's goodwill is close at hand,' Plato explains (in the voice of Socrates), '[the lover] realizes that all the friendship he has from his other friends and relatives put together is nothing compare to that of this friend who is inspired by a god.' They hug and kiss, and now they also develop a sense of 'bliss and shared understanding', This is a love that does not pass with the morning but that can shared into the sunset of their lives.

Badiou defines such erotic friendship as remaining committed to love. It is in fidelity to our beloved, especially when hot romance has abated, that mature love wins its victory. Only then do we grow up once again:

> While desire focuses on the other, always in a somewhat fetishist manner, on particular objects, like breasts, buttocks and cock, love focuses on the very being of the other, on the other as it has erupted, fully armed with its being, into my life that is consequently disrupted and refashioned.

Alain Badiou, with N. Truong, *In Praise of Love*
(London: Serpent's Tail, 2009)

The significance of this shift in romance is explored in Erich Fromm's analysis of love, too, in his book *The Art of Loving*. When two people meet, he notes, they are strangers. If they then suddenly feel close to one another, that leads to what can be the most exhilarating and exciting experience in life. The lost half is found. Surely this is it, they are bound to ask, or hope?

However, falling in love cannot last because it is premised on the meeting of strangers. Once this new other stops being delightfully strange to you, the feeling of falling in love eases off, too. The risk is that disappointment rushes in. Instead of delighting you, the beloved now irritates. Instead of bringing joy, the relationship elicits anxiety. Has not the love died?

At the time of falling in love, this was impossible to think about. Young Eros ruled. The intensity of the experience was the very measure of love's worth. Love was its own end. However, falling in love is just one element of love and not the whole story. The danger is that people become addicted to falling in love and its thrills. It leads to serial relationships, in succession or concurrently, and makes it hard to hold relationships down. Such a tendency does seem to be a feature of modern culture, one that has forgotten about Anteros, the grit in between the two who would become one. But a different kind of love is premised not on being locked together in a primitive dyad. It is about being known to each other as other. Fromm calls it 'standing in love'. To stand in love is to love a person whom you know, and who knows you.

Aristophanes' myth is only partly right. Romantic love feels as if it has a fearsome inevitability about it. Young lovers believe, at first, that they are made for each other, as if the stars had destined them to meet, or maybe as if they once knew each other in a former life. But now they come to see that their love is not best resourced by a mythical past, but sustained by an actual future, one worked at and worked out.

In many ways, this is a natural development. Relationships that last do so precisely because they shift from the romantic phase of falling in love to the maturity of standing in love. Or, in Badiou's language, they are able to cope with conflict and grow into deep but sensible commitments. Lovers that survive the transition feel as if they have come to their senses. This is a freer place to be when compared with the thrilling claustrophobia of romance.

This place is called friendship, a type of shared affection that introduces a further and once more dramatically different dimension to love's possibilities. Our exploration began with the love of one, and then opened up to dyadic love: love in twos. It must now push to another constellation if we are to understand this new mode. We are approaching the insight that love reaches its fullest maturity when it loves self, can reach out to another, and, most importantly, can also operate in triangles of three. First, though, there is a little bit more to say about sex.

4

An evolutionary interlude: What is sex for?

ALL THAT MATTERS

▶ The invention of sex

The word 'sexy' is less than a hundred years old. The phrase 'having sex' only became common currency during the Second World War. The poet Philip Larkin famously proposed that sexual intercourse began as recently as 1963.

The twentieth century might be thought of as a period of human history, probably not the first, when the discussion of sex eclipsed the discussion of love. The logic of evolution by natural selection can again be discerned in the way human relations are thought about. After Darwin, the meaning of erotic love became secondary to the purpose of the sexual act, namely the propagation of the species. As we noted above when discussing romance, love was reinterpreted as the emotional force that genes deploy to encourage couples to 'do it'. Making love came to mean having sex. As the philologist Owen Barfield noted: 'It is accordingly taken for granted in most quarters that the sexual instinct is the underlying reality and that what is called "love" is a late-come embroidery on it.'

Barfield wrote that in an introduction to an English translation of *The Meaning of Love* (1892) by Vladimir Solovyov. This nineteenth-century Russian philosopher was a great influence on those giant novelists of the human psyche and love, Dostoyevsky and Tolstoy. He presents another arresting counter-argument to the evolutionary subjugation of love to sex that seems so dominant in contemporary culture. Once more it suggests that there is every reason to believe that love inspires sex, not sex love.

Solovyov begins with a striking observation. In the natural word, sex actually has little to do with propagation. Many organisms in the plant and animal world reproduce by non-sexual means – by propagating, in fact, in the everyday sense: grafting, budding, parthenogenesis.

The truth is that sexual union as the key method of reproduction appears to be limited to the most socially complex organisms. For example, fish reproduce sexually, if not via a bodily union. Fish eggs are fertilized, typically on a massive scale, by a generous distribution of sperm ejected by males in the water outside the body of the female. No young fry knows who its dad is. Fish are cold-blooded, of course, and it is perhaps the combination of pretty complex social lives and carelessly uninhibited sexual promiscuity that explains the reason we use the phrase 'cold-blooded' to mean loveless, as well as lacking a capacity to heat the blood.

Birds typically have more complex social lives compared with fish and therefore, perhaps, appear to show some signs of what humans would call love. The faithfulness of the swan, say, is renowned in literature. Hence, we speak of 'love birds'.

But what is striking about animals as complex in behaviour as birds, Solovyov continues, is that their sexual union is relatively unproductive in terms of sheer numbers of offspring, particularly when compared to the swarming fry of the cold-blooded fish. On occasion, birds may raise young with no sexual union at all: same-sex swan pairs have been observed building nests. They steal eggs to raise cygnets together. More usually, love birds raise young, though no more than a handful. And they do not leave their offspring to be consumed in their millions, as fish do with fry.

The disconnection between sex and mass reproduction deepens as you move across the animal kingdom. The more love-like behaviour between animal pairs, the fewer are their issue. It does appear to be the case that having offspring seems to be hitching a ride on sexual activity, which arises with social complexity, rather than being the main driver for it. By the time you arrive at human beings, sexual love can often be almost completely separated from having children. For the human couple, sharing their lives together month by month, pregnancy is typically a highly inconvenient, if not disastrous, result of making love. The overwhelmingly dominant purpose of sex is not propagation. It is love – or, at least, should be. Solovyov concludes: '[A]t the two extremes of animal existence we find on the one hand propagation without any sexual love, and on the other hand sexual love without any propagation.' He concludes: '[I]t is perfectly clear that these two phenomena cannot be bonded indissolubly with one another.'

The unexpected conclusion is that the natural world itself suggests that the meaning of love cannot be based in the reproductive aspects of sex. Reproduction is a by-product, not the main purpose.

In fact, the origins of sexual reproduction remain something of mystery to science. The high priest of Darwinian evolution, Richard Dawkins, has returned the subject repeatedly in his books. He variously admits that biological explanations for sex are not 'knock-down convincing' and that 'no definitive verdict has emerged'. Sex just does not seem that efficient at spreading genes or nurturing the mutations that aid evolutionary adaptation. Neither is sexual display a particularly good way of selecting a potent partner. Though it is often talked about, the evidence that this takes place is weak. Why the peacock has such a wonderful tail, or why stags grow enormous antlers and rut, is unclear. Females do not appear much bothered. Little wonder Darwin himself felt that the meaning of sexual reproduction was 'hidden in darkness'.

In his recent survey of the subject, the science writer Michael Brooks turns to the pleasure sex gives as a possible alternative explanation. Writing in his book *13 Things That Don't Make Sense*, he wonders whether the joy of sex aids group bonding in socially complex animals. He does not call it love; biologists stick to the functionality of sex. But the hedonic thesis is possible. Creatures that mate often live in groups. Perhaps the tensions of living in groups are eased by the release afforded by mating? That is why propagation has little to do with it.

But is that plausible either? Is it not the case that erotic love frequently causes human beings problems? Worse, the more passionate the love, the less social harmony might ensue. Human love is often unrequited, causing profound loneliness and despair. When treated as a pleasure-delivering activity, sex is likely to break stable breeding pairs up, not bind them more firmly together.

As the philosopher Arthur Schopenhauer noted, in a similar vein:

> *[Sex] does not hesitate ... to interfere with the negotiations of statesmen and the investigations of the learned. It knows how to slip its love-notes and ringlets even into ministerial portfolios and philosophical manuscripts... It sometimes demands the sacrifice of ... health, sometimes of wealth, position and happiness.*

Arthur Schopenhauer, *The World as Will and Representation*, vol. 2 (New York: Dover Publications, 1966), pp. 533–4

Sex, at least when it comes to humans, looks to be the opposite of a successful survival strategy.

▶ The spiritual meaning of sex

It may be more productive simply to drop attempts to understand sexual love biologically. Solovyov, for one, believes that where science fails, ethics provides an answer. The worth of sexual love, he argues, is found not in any generational necessity, but in the flourishing of the individual. Sexual love can be understood when it is seen to have subjective and spiritual meaning.

The starting point for this analysis is human egoism, the ethical word for narcissism. Our ego tells us that we – I – am of supreme significance. And this is quite right. It is the function of narcissism again or, to put it in more ethical terms, it is a fundamental insight of theistic and secular ethics that the human person is of infinite worth. The principle is enshrined in modern human rights and in the doctrine that the individual is made in the image of God. In every person, there is something that is irreplaceable, unique. They literally cannot be valued too highly and so human beings should not be used as a means to an end, but as ends in themselves.

So why, then, does egoism have such a bad write-up in ethics? Why does it carry connotations of vanity and conceit? The answer is that the awareness of one's own value so often leads to the denial of the worth of others. If you put yourself at the centre of the universe, it is very easy to push others to the periphery. 'The basic falsehood and evil of egoism lie not in this absolute self-consciousness and self-evaluation of the subject,' Solovyov writes, 'but in the fact that, ascribing to himself in all justice an absolute significance, he unjustly refuses to others this same significance.' This is another way of describing the dangers of narcissism and why it must be transcended.

The denial is particularly powerful at a psychological, inner level. The law protects the rights of others 'out there'. But internally – in numerous secret feelings of grandiosity, hate and anger; and in the little everyday deeds that escape the opprobrium of the law – we routinely discount the absolute worth of others. So, living as if others mattered unconditionally demands nothing less than a personal transformation. It is a lifelong spiritual task.

A key element in that is the gradual realization that there is no absolute boundary between ourselves and others. We are in life together from the start. Everyone comes from someone. No man is an island – again, this is a truth that must be *felt*, not just known as a fact. Further, because our separate existence is also a collective existence, it is only with others that we can fulfil our potential as unique individuals of absolute worth. The individual who tries to assert him- or herself without regard for others, or at the expense of others, has embarked on a fruitless task. Their 'success' will be empty, their life divested of meaning.

Solovyov argues that sexual love plays a special role in tackling the excesses of egoism. True love demands that we recognize another, he explains. In love, we transfer the centre of our life to another. We then live not only in our own life but in another's life. The sexual element is vital because its bodily passion means we undeniably sense the truth of our connection with another. Our flesh tells us that we need them. Feeling requires that interpenetrative fullness. Sexual desire will have it no other way.

Other kinds of love speak similarly, though with less power. Platonic friendship lacks the erotic element – though perhaps the closest kinds of friendship are those that do contain an erotic element, either the erotic friendship that emerges with standing in love or a friendship that is never expressed sexually because its erotic, passionate nature is sublimated. The love between a parent and child is not between equals and parents must give more. Mystical love lacks the concreteness of an actual lover. In patriotism and the love of country, the individual loses their sense of themselves in the collective, it is true. But the point is that '[i]n order genuinely to undermine egoism, it is necessary to oppose to it a love equally concretely specific, permeating the whole of our being and taking possession of everything in it.' Sex can do that. Solovyov continues:

> Only under the action of this, so to speak, chemical union of two beings, of the same nature and of equal significance, but on all sides distinct as to form, is the creation possible (both in the natural order and in the spiritual order) of a new human being, the real realization of true human individuality. Such a union, or at least the closest approximation to it, we find in sexual love, for which reason we attach to it exceptional significance.

> V. Solovyov, *The Meaning of Love*, trans. Thomas R. Beyer and introd. Owen Barfield (Herndon, VA: Lindisfarne Press, 1985), p. 46

This vision of sexual love as something needed to overcome egoism is not Solovyov's alone. It reaches back at least to Plato, who argued that it is only erotic desire that can irresistibly awaken us to the existence of others and of our connection to them. Lovers, he proposes in the *Phaedrus*, spend a 'blessed life wandering around in the light with one another'.

Of course, sexual love can be abusive. It may deny the reality of the other. Perhaps more often than not, in trying to oppose tyrannical egoism, it loses out and the egoism reigns, meaning the sexual possession of one by another, not a connection of two. But Solovyov argues that this failure is no reason to give up on the meaning of sexual love. It is characteristic of human beings to fall short on the qualities that might give life meaning. We are never wholly rational, conscious, wise, just, free or happy. Why think we would be any more perfect when it comes to the ideals of sexual loving?

Is three a crowd?

Immature love says: 'I love you because I need you.' Mature love says: 'I need you because I love you.'

Erich Fromm

ALL THAT MATTERS

▶ Oedipal trouble

The ancient story of Oedipus, the king of Thebes who unwittingly married his mother and killed his father, has become notorious, almost two and a half thousand years after the story was told by Sophocles. Freud latched on to the myth as expressing a wish that all people have at some level of their being. The way in which we work out how to live with our parents, and *not* 'marry' one and 'destroy' the other, profoundly shapes our inner lives and our capacity to love, he thought.

It is a shocking notion. Little wonder Freud was so anxious about how his key idea would be received and Oedipal love has been passionately critiqued ever since. That said, close observers of family life and love might be prepared to recognize that there is something in it. Lisa Appignanesi, writing in her book *All About Love*, describes the moment she realized Freud was right, at least in part:

> One day when [my son] was about four and I was driving him home from nursery, he adamantly demanded a pair of scissors. 'What for?' I asked him, from the front seat of the car. 'I need them,' he insisted, and when I probed once more, he announced he needed them for his Dad, eventually revealing, before bursting into peals of laughter, that he needed them to cut off his Dad's willy. After a momentary sense of shock, I assured him that that was hardly a good idea, and of course, by the time we'd got home he'd forgotten all about it. He greeted his father in the ordinary way

and went off merrily to dismantle some robotic monster instead.

Lisa Appignanesi, *All about Love: Anatomy of an Unruly Emotion* (London: Virago, 2011), p. 276

Another example is the time I was with the children of some friends, two brothers and a sister, aged about nine, seven and five. We were all having dinner, and the young girl momentarily choked on a spaghetti hoop. Before her father could reach out to help her, her brothers had begun to chorus: 'Die, die, die!' They are not nasty boys at all. And yet, in that moment an Oedipal competition spontaneously surfaced between them. It was as if, at some level, they assumed that one less sibling would mean one less individual with whom to fight for love. Interestingly, and like Lisa Appignanesi's son, the three kids all burst into peels of laughter after the moment of aggression had passed. It felt as if a feeling, normally repressed as a taboo, had been vented. The hilarity was in relief.

Another sign of Oedipal trouble might come when an individual recognizes that their search for a lover as an adult is not so much a search for a lover as for a parent, one perhaps loved ambivalently at first and now sought virtually, in order to be reconciled with them. Many people will have a friend who seems to have married a close replica of their opposite-sex parent. Some will occasionally allow themselves the unsteadying thought that there is something about their own partner that secretly reminds them of their father or mother, too.

The journalist Liz Hoggard has written movingly about the loss of her father ('the first man in your life'). In an article for the British daily newspaper the *Daily Mail*, she writes:

> *Born in the 1930s my father lived through the War; there was little time for luxury or sentiment. In my teenage years we had arguments. He found me chaotic and impractical. My reaction was to look for men who judged me less strictly. But actually I kept dating men who were uncannily similar to my father. They kept me at arm's length when I got upset or insecure.*

Liza Hoggard, *Mail Online*, 9 July 2012 (http://m.dailymail.
co.uk/mobile/femail/article.html?articleID=2170697)

▶ Love's loss

Of course, normal human development is precisely not about indulging the fearful impulses of patricide and incest. It is about how individuals move from the love in a pair with mother, which was so delightful and necessary, to a wider love that can embrace third parties, be that father or siblings, or more generally, new people, new possibilities and new experiences. This is the challenge. It is a third kind of love, a mode that can love not only self and one other, but emotionally all that life might bring.

So today psychotherapists tend not to think about this stage of development narrowly in terms of the secret desires for mother and murderous intent against father. Instead, the Oedipal situation refers to the period when the child first begins to sense that it will not always be able to have the one other it loves and longs for solely for itself.

It may well be that a first taste of this loss comes when the child's mother is not exclusively available. Or when it realizes that mother has other loves, too, not least father but perhaps also her work, or time for herself, or her other children. The child senses that some human beings love each other in ways that differ from the love it experiences and knows. It begins to sense that mother loves father – or work, or the other kids – with a slightly different quality from the way she loves him or her. Her voice sounds a bit different when she talks with him. Their mutuality is marked by laughter or grunts, not the calm cooing and ga-ga noises the child knows and loves. Perhaps they are sharing something secret, a suspicion that might be confirmed later when the parents talk in code or spell words out so that their child is kept in the dark. They don't say 'play park' but P-L-A-Y-P-A-R-K. Similarly, they say not 'sex', but S-E-X.

▶ Other Oedipal myths

Freud was not the first to explore the troubled feelings in families that children feel towards their parents and siblings as they struggle with love. It is a staple of folk stories and fairy tales.

[*The Gingerbread Woman comes out of the house and speaks.*]

▲ Illustration for *Hansel and Gretel* from a 1911 US children's book by Florence Holbrook. The abandoned children meet the witch at the gingerbread house.

Snow White tells the story of a beautiful princess born to a queen who dies. Her father, the king, gets remarried to a vain stepmother who is always asking her mirror: who is the fairest? You are, the mirror replies – and all seems well until Snow White reaches the age of seven, that is, she moves from infancy into girlhood, anticipating womanhood.

Now Snow White is fairer and her stepmother cannot bear the thought that she will be surpassed by her stepdaughter. She tries to kill Snow White who is successively saved by a huntsman, seven dwarves and finally a prince. It is painful separation from her family of origin, the Oedipal element, that finally allows Snow White to live.

As for the stepmother, who symbolically carries all the difficult feelings in this family, she is forced into a pair of hot iron shoes, and dances until she dies.

Hansel and Gretel is the story of how a brother and sister survive the loss of their mother, the schemes of their stepmother, and the plans of a witch to eat them. That all three 'mothers' die suggests that they are different aspects of the same parent as experienced by the children. First their real mother dies, as if the story is telling us that at some point even the good mother will let you down. Indeed, she must, if you are to grow.

Then the stepmother treats them cruelly, believing that she must be with the father in a relationship of two in order to thrive. This is a symbolic representation of the way the mother might be experienced as flawed or hurtful.

Then the witch, who lives in the gingerbread house – a home so nourishing you can eat it – tries to eat them. Perhaps this captures some of the difficulties children face in the give and take of growing up.

Then again, the witch is wealthy and the children eventually live happily on what she leaves behind. This third version of mother is a tricky, though indispensable, object.

Hamlet, the play by Shakespeare, relates the struggles of a Danish prince to avenge the death of his father, whom he believes has been killed by his uncle. Shakespeare heaps various interpretations of Hamlet's predicament into his text, as any good mythmaker would. But one way of reading it, picked up by Freud, is to suggest that Hamlet worries about avenging his father's death because, in his barely conscious Oedipal fantasies, he has killed his father already. It is therefore he, not his uncle, who deserves to die. He is driven possibly mad with guilt.

Hamlet is also tormented by his mother's remarriage to his uncle. He declares that he wants to free his mother from this incestuous coupling, though possibly because of the incestuous feelings he has himself. He is certainly obsessed with the sexual nature of his mother's new relationship. 'In the rank sweat of an enseamed bed. / Stew'd in corruption...', he spits at her (Act III, scene iv, lines 100–101). Again, it could be argued that he projects his Oedipal guilt on to others, his mother as well as his uncle, because his inner feelings of loss and longing are too disturbing for him to bear by himself.

Helping us through this transition is the purpose of the stable nuclear family. The mother–child–father family unit can be critiqued in many ways – for the pressure it places on just two parents in the raising of children, for its patriarchal pattern, for its exclusionary claustrophobia. And yet, if it is thought of as describing a minimal requirement for the child, it makes sense. The infant needs mother to get started in the world, the person who is at first devoted to it. Then it needs to grow beyond that tight partnership of concern so that it can love others. Dad, or the third person in the family, is arguably the most straightforward way of providing a necessary interruption into the world of the cosy twosome. He breaks into the dyad. It is difficult for the child, as are all recognitions that love is less contained and controlled than was first thought. Though life can also, therefore, become bigger. As Graham Greene observed in his novel *The Power and the Glory*: 'There is always one moment in childhood when the door opens and lets the future in.'

As with the previous transitions, these traumas have to be tolerated by the child. If the twist away from the parental bosom is not bearable, then reality may come to be experienced as persecutory – as if life is out to get the child. But if the child can embrace the fact that its primary carer loves another, too, then another expansion of its world takes place. From the vantage of its own love for Mother, it can see that she loves another, and it can share in this love as well. Life is no longer just determined by the love between two people, but now takes on a triangular formation. More permutations are possible in threesomes. Life becomes richer and more exciting as reality opens up.

▶ Triangular space

The psychotherapist Ronald Britton calls this 'triangular space'. He notes that it contains a further, crucial feature. The child can now *observe* two other people loving one another, and also can come to know that it is observed by another when it loves Mother. The power of this capacity for observing life, as well as participating in life, can hardly be underestimated. It is arguably the quality that makes us most fully human.

In his essay 'The missing link: parental sexuality in the Oedipus complex', Britton writes: 'The capacity to envisage a benign parental relationship influences the development of a space outside the self – capable of being observed and thought about, which provides the basis for a belief in a secure and stable world.' In much the same way that a tripod is steadier than a one- or two-legged table, so the experience of life when connected to more than one other person creates a greater sense of existential resilience and reliability, too.

To be an observer of love, as well as a participant, means that the child begins to develop the ability to steady itself, emotionally and psychologically. It no longer needs to respond spontaneously to things. It can pause, consider the options, and then act. It begins to entertain other points of view, to see things as others might see them, to try out how it might react before actually reacting. Infantile emotions are moderated. Other more mature emotions are toyed with. It begins to grow up and reason starts to have a bearing on the complex negotiations of the everyday.

This is to say that the child develops the capacity for that inner flexibility called self-consciousness. Triangular space, with its associated feelings of trust and resilience as well as desire for openness and newness, provides the ground from which the individual can engage in lateral thinking, and move beyond the literal and concrete. In a child exploring the possibilities of love in mode three, you see suspicion giving way to curiosity, defensiveness to openness. Love conquers fear.

Again, it feels difficult at first. Being self-conscious means being exposed to the possibilities of being embarrassed, feeling exposed, anticipating trouble. Many parents witness a moment when their child, perhaps around the age of five or six, shifts from being happy playing the fool before them, like a paid entertainer, to bursting into tears, apparently without reason, because it suddenly fears it is not being laughed with but laughed at.

This is the shock of the third place, an inner sense of separation that comes with self-awareness. The child has caught a glimpse of the amusement at its antics that the parents share as adults, and its childish part momentarily feels cast out, unbalanced, excluded. However, if the parent can comfort the child, the child will come to trust the capacity for self-awareness. It will grow in the skills of observing and add them to its repertoire of loves.

▶ Embracing the whole story

This more open-ended love is implicit in the Oedipus myth, too. He is the man who has become king because he is apparently knowledgeable. He solved the Riddle of the Sphinx: 'What is the creature that moves on four legs

▲ Jean-Auguste-Dominique Ingres, *Oedipus and the Sphinx*, oil on canvas, 1808.

in the morning, two at noon, and three in the evening?'
'Man – who crawls on all fours as a baby, walks on two feet as an adult, and then walks with a cane in old age,' Oedipus replied, thereby solving the riddle and making the Sphinx destroy herself, relieving the city of Thebes from attacks by the lion–human hybrid. There is also his name, which does not just mean 'swollen-foot' but which also, as it sounds in Greek, carries echoes of 'know-foot'.

But the knowledge Oedipus has of himself and life is limited. It turns out that the Sphinx is not just referring to human beings in general, but to Oedipus in particular. When he finds out that he killed his own father and had children by his mother, he blinds himself, and needs a stick to find his way. He understood only part of the riddle and took that understanding to be the whole.

This is the troubling lesson he learns, in Sophocles' story. It shows that, just when we think we have grasped life, it turns out that our perceptions are imperfect, our understanding incomplete. A true love of life must be being able to cope with the *whole story*, whatever its truths. Oedipus' wife and mother, Jocasta, cannot face it. She kills herself when she discovers the full truth. Horror and fear destroy the love that might keep her in life. Oedipus blinds himself, as if to show that surface appearances are deceiving. He is a tragic hero because, although he now understands that his knowledge was partial, he loves life enough to stay alive in spite of the pain.

Another way of putting this is to say that growing up demands an awareness of the distance that exists between people as well as the intimacy. Dyadic love cannot be the whole story but must be interrupted, forcing a look elsewhere. Again, though, it is a hopeful move because looking ahead reveals that there is somewhere else to look, into the world and life. Mature love equips us to make this move.

We are in the domain of Anteros once more, supplemented by the insights of the Oedipal myth. An ideal of relationships in tight twos must die because being seamlessly joined does not make for adult human flourishing. We must be able to bear our differences as well as similarities; to become more than two, not two collapsing into one. Lovers, like a mother and child, must not only gaze into each other's eyes to thrive. They must look ahead into their future. Passion is first stirred, and must then be expanded into a passion for life. As an adult couple, a *joie de vivre* develops. It invites others in, as opposed to keeping intruders out. You can spot couples who have achieved this ability to stand in love because they are so good to be with. Their love bids you – a third – welcome.

A painful interlude:
Love's knowledge

▶ The educated heart

The pain of love's transitions has been a constant theme. But now, with the dynamics of inner triangular space, we can develop it further. What I am thinking of has been called 'love's knowledge' by the philosopher Martha Nussbaum and she draws on what Aristotle called the 'educated heart'.

Nussbaum finds a classic account of such insight in Proust's novel *À la recherche du temps perdu* (In Search of Lost Time). There is a moment in the story when Marcel, the main character, realizes that he loves Albertine. But here's the twist: he only knows that he loves her when she has left him. He hadn't been troubled by the prospect of being without her up to that point. He thought he was indifferent to her. And yet, when his heart, as opposed to his head, is stirred by her leaving, an entirely different perception of the situation breaks in and overwhelms him. He can think of little else but her. Proust provides a record of Marcel's thoughts:

> *My imagination sought her in the skies, on evenings like those when we were still able to gaze at it together; I tried to wing my affections towards her, beyond the moonlight that she loved, to console her for no longer being alive, and this love for a person who had become so remote was like a religion, my thoughts rose toward her like prayers.*

Marcel Proust, *In Search of Lost Time*, vol. 5, trans. C.K. Scott Moncrieff, T. Kilmartin and D.J. Enright (London: Modern Library Edition), p. 690

▲ Marcel Proust understood the thrills of romantic love, though he was also a pessimist about love's promise.

It's a familiar experience. Parting makes the heart grow fonder, it is said. Only Proust pushes his examination of the platitude a stage further, and this reveals a different insight. When Marcel starts to tell his friends and acquaintances about his loss, he simultaneously realizes that his sadness at losing her is already lessening. His heart is telling his head something else he didn't know.

For example, one evening the duchesse de Guermantes invites him to the opera. He remembers Albertine and so, as if by habit, declines:

> But I replied sadly: 'No, I cannot go to the theatre, I have lost a friend. She was very dear to me.' The tears nearly came to my eyes as I said it and yet for the first time I felt something akin to pleasure in talking about it. It was from that moment that I started to write to everyone to tell them of my great sorrow and to cease to feel it.

Marcel Proust, *In Search of Lost Time*, vol. 5, trans. C.K. Scott Moncrieff, T. Kilmartin and D.J. Enright (London: Modern Library Edition)

He has the capacity to *observe* his feelings, not just to *have* them.

▶ The wisdom of pain

It might also be called a training and refinement of feeling, and this was something the novelist E.M. Forster was interested in, too. Many of his characters only gain a true understanding of what the good life consists in when they have discarded what they thought they knew about it. Typically, it is love that explodes their delusions and, though the experience is painful, a distance from the immediacy of a troubled situation opens up and they become much wiser about life as a result.

In *A Room with a View*, Forster describes how Lucy Honeychurch has just such an awakening when she realizes she is in love with George. For most of the novel she won't allow herself to acknowledge the fact because she thinks she knows her mind on the matter. She thinks she does not love George, but Cecil. She is refusing to observe the wisdom of her heart and, as a result, Forster writes:

> *She gave up trying to understand herself, and joined the vast armies of the benighted, who follow neither the heart nor the brain, and march to their destiny by catchwords. The armies are full of pleasant and pious folk. But they have yielded to the only enemy that matters – the enemy within. They have sinned against passion and the truth, and vain will be their strife after virtue.*

E.M. Forster, *A Room with a View* (Mineola, NY: Dover Thrift Editions, 1995), p. 143

Forster describes how such individuals become cynical, hypocritical and uncomfortable with life. But Lucy is lucky, though she does not think so at the time. A new insight bursts upon her because, like Marcel, she comes to her wits' end. This time the breakdown is precipitated by Mr Emerson, George's father, who tells her that she will never know beauty and passion unless she acknowledges that she loves George. In an instant, Lucy sees it and, luckily for her, she has just enough self-awareness not to ignore it. She tries to understand herself again. Love's knowledge enables this to happen.

Friendship and belonging

Opposition is true friendship.

William Blake

▶ Making friends

Close friendship becomes possible with the emergence of love's third dimension because friendship is a relationship with this psychological shape too. It first becomes an issue in the family, when parents encourage their children to be friends, not just Oedipal rivals. But the child itself perhaps first becomes obsessed with the importance of friendship when it goes to school. It takes the love it has internalized within the family and deploys it to survive in this new place.

The new psychic space of the playground and classroom is marked by a constant testing of the limits and rules of friendship, of how to relate to these strange others. Gangs form. Bonds are sealed by swapping secrets or Pokemon cards. A child of this age is deeply sensitive to who is in and who out. Bullying is so devastating, perhaps scarring for life, because unchecked it embeds the belief that the love called friendship is not to be trusted. Children can be sweet to one another and a moment later shockingly vile because they are stress-testing friendship – gaining a sense of how it bends and where it snaps. It is invaluable knowledge for later life, when winning friends and influencing people becomes a crucial skill.

The psychotherapist Mary Waddell, in her book *Inside Lives*, notes:

> *The family relationships, even though they are still central to the child's world, nonetheless begin to loosen slightly to include, for example, wider*

> friendships, the school day, perhaps also brief stays
> elsewhere. The success or otherwise with which
> these social tasks may be accomplished depends to
> some extent on the degree to which the emotional
> ferment which has preceded them is felt to have
> been, and to be, under control.

Mary Waddell, *Inside Lives: Psychoanalysis and the Growth of the Personality* (New York: Routledge, 1998), p. 74

Erotic passions tend to be less demonstrative during this time. Developmentally, it is known as the latency period. It is often said that children of this age are at their most delightful. They are having a first stab at friendship before the psychosexual trauma picks up once more during their teenage years. It is as if learning something about friendship now equips the child, so that later, as a teenager, it may make the move from falling to standing in love. Early lessons in friendship well absorbed resource us to be open to love's more mature forms, so a capacity for friendship is a key, fundamental, part of love. After all, who would say life was good if they had no friend?

▶ Friendship types

So what is the essential nature of friendship? Aristotle argued that there are different types. One type of friendship forms because the friends are useful to each other. It may be work colleagues, or college mates, or individuals who enjoy the same interests or pleasures. The point is that they share the goodwill called friendship because they get something – a third thing – out of being together. When that good thing disappears, perhaps the collegiality of work because one person changes jobs or an interest formerly shared wanes, the friendship dissolves, too. This kind of friendship lasts only as long as the shared element lasts. Take that away and the relationship collapses.

A second type of friendship is triangular as well. The difference is that the good thing that these friends share is not an external utility or pleasure. They love each other not for something outside of themselves, like work or an interest. They love each other for who they are in themselves and for the life they therefore know together. It may be their depth of character, their innate goodness, their intensity of passion or their simple *joie de vivre*, but once established on such a basis these friendships are ones that will last. Nothing can be taken away from it. We say these friends are 'soul mates' or 'best friends'.

What this adds up to is that, if the love shared in families has much to do with wanting to *care* for others, and the love shared by romantic lovers is primarily one that longs to *have* another, then the love shared by friends is one that along with everything else longs to *know* another, and be known by them. It is that quality that makes friendship the most open-ended kind of love. Friends want to know each other by sharing the experiences of life with one another – a crucially different kind of sharing from lovers in the first flush of romance who simply want to be with each other. Lovers may later want to become erotic friends, too, in order that they may do the same.

This explains why the characteristic activity of good friendship is talking. The act of talking, face-to-face, is the way that friends get to know each other through their shared experience. When good friends have been apart, they say things like: 'We picked up just where we left off: it is as if we had never stopped talking.'

Aristotle also thought that the best kind of friends know each other as 'another self'. It is another demonstration of the way in which friendship becomes possible in tandem with self-awareness. A close friend performs the same function, becoming a kind of mirror of your own self, someone with whom you find personal resonances and dissonances. It is not going too far to say that human beings probably know themselves best in the context of friendship. You see something of yourself in your friend; you sense how you are different. All the while, you know you are not alone. You realize that there is someone else who is quite like you and who you quite like.

Therein lies much of friendship's delight: friendship is such a vital aspect of human love because in friendship we know that we belong *and* that we are adults. As tiny infants, we felt the world belonged to us. We feel we belong to another, when in our mother or lover's arms. Friendship builds on these experiences and adds another dimension. It promises that we can be ourselves fully as separate individuals and at the same time know ourselves as belonging with others. It is the fullest flourishing of human love in a blend of autonomy and dependence.

▲ The Old Testament friends David and Jonathan, here depicted in a nineteenth-century illustrated Bible, represent the ideal of friendship.

▶ Self-love

There is an interesting link between the capacity for friendship and narcissistic love, too, because deep friendship is only possible when an individual has learned to befriend him- or herself. Naturally enough, people usually talk about friendship in terms of a relationship with someone else. Friends spend time together, wish well for each other, share joys and sorrows, or are simply glad their friend exists. But friendship also depends upon the relationship one has with oneself. We need a certain friendship with ourselves to live happily. Someone who likes spending time with themselves, wishes well for themselves, can embrace their own joys and sorrows, and is glad to be alive – all the things that friends share – is more likely to be a good friend, too. In psychological terms, they need to have developed the kind of love that means they are comfortable in their own skin.

Aristotle would agree. He argues that good self-love comes before being able to form friendships with others. The person who cannot befriend themselves is not likely to make friends with others. They will be preoccupied and obsessed with themselves.

Similarly, there is the kind of self-love that motivates someone to want to be better. If someone wants to lead well, parent well, work well or write well – that is, become a better person in some way – will they not first have to love themselves? It is implicit in the desire to better oneself. These people are also likely to benefit others because of their self-love – in leading, parenting, working or writing. They will have a capacity to offer rewarding friendship. In fact, the good friend will be a good self-lover, in this sense too, Aristotle says. And paradoxically, they will do so selflessly, in a spirit of service. Because they love themselves enough to get over themselves, they will give what they have achieved or received back from those around them. Ralph Waldo Emerson caught the dynamic well when he observed that, if you want to *have* a friend, then *be* a friend.

To put it the other way round, there is a kind of self-love that is selfish and thwarts friendship. It is the love that grasps things for itself. Such individuals assign themselves the larger share of money, of honour, of pleasure. The friends of such people will know it because they will feel used and excluded.

▶ How much time should we spend with friends?

Is once a year enough, with intermediary emails and calls? Once a month? Once a week? Daily?

It is a question that niggles. The challenge is a serious one, for so many things in modern life can take us away from friends. Work, marriage, opportunities and thinking the grass is greener elsewhere can take us from them and them from us. Little wonder that there is plenty of evidence that loneliness is a common feature of modern life. It is not that people live in isolation on the whole. It is that quite often the quality of their contact with the people around them is poor. If you are not careful, you can end up with many friends to do stuff with and to enjoy stuff with, but when it comes to sharing in the most intimate ways, is there anyone there?

Aristotle's message is *invest*. Unless maintained, friendship diminishes over time. 'Cut off the talk, and many a time you cut off the friendship' was his way of summing it up. He believed that friends will naturally want to live together, not necessarily under the same roof but in terms of sharing the ins and outs of daily life.

When they cannot, they will feel something is missing. And if they do not for a very long period of time, then the affection will weaken. It is as if the friends forget why they were friends. They change. They make other friends. They wish each other well, but no longer need the friendship day by day.

This is to say that the energy in friendship comes from life and the future, not the past. It is another reflection on the observation that lovers look into each other's eyes, whereas friends look ahead. Good friends have a life together ahead of them. That third perspective is what fires the relationship and deepens the love.

Old friends have a life behind them, of course, and they will reminisce on it, nostalgically. However, they will draw down on that store of relational energy, and, much as a battery eventually goes flat, so also will a friendship that attempts to live solely in the past. The stories become boring, the reminiscing a trap.

How many friends can one person have?

The answer is remarkably precise, at least according to evolutionary science. The anthropologist Robin Dunbar has done the maths, made the measurements. It turns out that the number of friendships one person can sustain is 150. It is known as 'Dunbar's number'. This is the size social groups should be, based upon the size of the human neocortex. Moreover, it turns out that the number 150 is about the size of many social groupings, from medieval villages to Roman cohorts.

I suspect a number appeals because of the utilitarian nature of modern culture. We like things to be *for* something, including friendship. It is as if you can't just *be* a friend. You must be a friend for a reason, a purpose. But this instrumental approach has knock-on effects. It subtly moves from being a description to a prescription – as if any happy *Homo sapiens needs* 150 friends or acquaintances.

Quantity is a perfectly sensible measure when buying apples at the supermarket. But we have a different relationship with people. They are I–Thou relationships, as the philosopher Martin Buber put it, not I–It, as the quantitative assessment makes them. Turn an I–Thou into an I–It, and you kill friendship stone dead. It's love by cost–benefit analysis, agony aunt advice from accountants. My friends are the service providers in my optimized life.

Aristotle thought differently. You might sum up his opinion with the expression 'Less is more'. 'Host not many, but host not none' is his formula. Friendliness is always good. But when it comes to intimate friendship you get the impression that he probably counted his friends on one hand, probably two at most. Intimacy in joy and grief can only be profoundly shared with a relative few. Close friendship requires that people have acquired experience with each other. Quality wins out over quantity.

It is useful, indeed necessary, to have some friends. So friendship does have instrumental value. There is something right about asking how many friends I need to have. The danger zone is the terrain between wanting to be useful to a friend and not wanting to feel used by that friend. The difference is felt very sharply. You know it immediately you start to feel like a service provider in your friend's life.

This then is a warning in our mobile days. Friendship is not like a family connection. To be friends with someone you have to be active. The decision must be sustained and reciprocated. It must be outward-looking. With family, you have no choice. That can be a blessing, as well as a curse, for family can always be called upon, even when you are loath to do so. But, if friendship is a choice, rather than something given, then it will require effort on the part of the friends. When it comes to the time you should spend with friends, more is more.

▶ The shadow of belonging

As always with love, its highest possibilities can lead unchecked to its deepest shadows. Friendship is no different and its ambivalent character has been worked out in great detail by the psychotherapist Bert Hellinger. He describes it in relation to what he calls conscience.

Hellinger does not mean conscience in the sense of an inner voice telling us what is right and wrong, but rather conscience in the sense of the feeling telling us what we must do or believe to belong. Therein lies the shadow because the desire and need to belong can readily eclipse the sense of right and wrong. 'A clear or a guilty conscience [in this revised sense] has little to do with good and evil; the worst atrocities and injustices are committed with a clear conscience, and we feel quite guilty doing good when it deviates from what others expect of us,' he explains in his book *Love's Hidden Symmetries* (p. 3).

Similarly, he argues that feeling innocent has little to do with doing the right thing, at least in the first instance. Instead, it comes from feeling that you belong because you are behaving as the collective will of your group requires. It is experienced as a kind of freedom because the person who finds their place with others by following others experiences an expansion of their life. They feel friendly towards and befriended by the group. Such love can provoke individuals to do great good and great evil.

Hellinger, a German, was writing in the aftermath of the Second World War, when ordinary citizens were complicit in terrible deeds because of a kind of civic friendship or comradeship that followed these rules of belonging. This powerful compulsion to belong explains how that could be so, or to put it in more common parlance, during times of war people on both sides will kill, sacrifice, and fight for love of their fellow men and country. The collective cause is *their* cause. This is the dark side of friendship.

The dynamic also sheds light on why individuals behave in different ways and even become slightly different people depending on whom they are with. A man might josh with his father, be submissive with his mother, be aggressive at work, be matey with his friends, be careless towards his wife and children. He acts and feels differently in these different contexts because that is what he imagines each group elicits from him.

▶ Collective conscience

Hellinger also discusses a deeper kind of conscience that is generally not felt, which he calls 'systemic conscience'. This is the belonging that arises because we are linked to previous generations in our family, circle or culture, even when we did not know these individuals personally. Again it is very powerful, subtly shaping our behaviour. I recently heard a man speak of his great-grandfather and tears sprang into his eyes, in spite of the fact that his beloved forebear died when he was just months old and he had no conscious memory of him.

Similarly, you may have noticed how corporations and businesses have dramatically different organizational characteristics, often conveyed in the brand. I worked for a while as a business journalist and visited lots of offices. It was possible to sense something of the personality of the organization just by walking into the reception. Employees tended to behave according to that collective personality, too – in what they wear, how they conduct themselves in the office, when they leave their personal ethics at the door. It is why a so-called 'clash of cultures' can bring even a great company down. It was as if the presence of the founders was still in the air. The organization was a system into which employees unconsciously fitted themselves.

We may say that this aspect of love is like the air we breathe. Though we hardly notice, it similarly sustains and feeds us. It was there before we were born and will survive our departure, though it will be changed a little by the inhalations and exhalations of our own lives. Freud described becoming an individual as a psychological achievement because an individual is someone who has negotiated the welter of affective pressures and forces that fill the environment into which he or she is born. We are caught in love's web, for good or ill, and we become who we are mostly in response to those who are physically and psychically close to us. It begins in our families, extends to our friends, and is filled out by the circles that make up the communities and organizations, the society and culture in which we live. We need each other to be *anybody* at all, though the paradox is that this makes it difficult to be *somebody*, too.

8

A third interlude:
Is love a feeling?

ALL THAT
MATTERS

▶ A sentimental journey

It seems a natural assumption to make. The great medieval writer Sir Thomas Malory is far from alone in complaining that 'the joy of love is too short' and its sorrow 'over long'. This is treating love as a feeling, a sentiment. But is that right? In a paper somewhat dauntingly entitled 'The conceptual framework for the investigation of emotions', the Oxford philosopher Peter Hacker points out that the word 'feeling' has so many meanings that it is tricky to know exactly what we mean when we say love is such an emotion.

For example, some feelings can be *perceptions*. If I pick up a hot plate, touch the damp earth, or play with an elastic band, then this is to gain information about something that is tangible. The plate is hot, the earth damp, the elastic band stretchy. These tactile feelings inform us about concrete things. We use a part of our body to find out about the world around us. We don't do that with love.

Such tactile perceptions are not the same as the feelings that we have *in* our bodies. Think of what it is to feel a pain or an itch. You do not use a part of your body to experience that, as you do the hot plate or damp earth. They are already felt in the body. Hence, to feel a pain is the same as being in pain. To feel an itch is the same as having an itch. Pain, itches and the like, then, are not perceptions but *sensations*, Hacker continues. And love is not quite like either.

A third category of feelings is *appetites*. These are feelings of hunger, thirst or lust. Appetites are different again from perceptions and sensations, though they may involve both. A grumble in the stomach, a dryness in the throat or a swelling sensation in the loins are prompts to satisfy an appetite. And this is the distinguishing characteristic of appetites because, when the appetite is satisfied, the sensation disappears – at least for a while. And, again, love does not work like that.

The fourth kind of feelings are *affections*. The quality that distinguishes affections from appetites, sensations and perceptions is that they do not tell you anything about your body or the world around you. Instead, they tell you about your inner psychic state. So your stomach may turn with fear or your heart sing for joy, but the fear does not tell you about the state of your stomach, or the joy your heart. It is the other way around. Your stomach speaks of your fear, your heart of your joy.

Love falls into this category. It is a type of affection. More specifically, Hacker argues that it is an *emotion*, though of a particular sort.

Love is not an appetite because it cannot be localized to a particular sensation in your body as appetites can. You may feel your stomach turn, you throat go dry, your loins warm when you are in love, but it makes little sense to say that you feel love in your stomach, throat or loins.

Another difference between love and appetites is that love has a specific target, whereas appetites do not. You may feel hungry for food or thirsty for a drink or lustful for a body. Yet when you love, you do not feel love for any man or woman, but specifically for the individual called Beth or Bert.

A third difference is that the intensity of the sensations associated with love is not an accurate measure of the intensity of the love. Love may lead to a flurry of feelings, but the mother who loves her child may often feel very little in spite of organizing her entire day so as to care for her little one. Her behaviour is the truer sign of her love. Similarly, the couple who have been together for 50 years may hardly notice how they feel in each other's presence, and yet, when one of them dies, the other is quietly broken-hearted and passes away just a few weeks later, too. That is a much more eloquent sign of their love than heightened sensations.

This makes love different from hunger or thirst because the level of hunger or thirst you feel is directly linked to the intensity of your need for food or a drink. With love, though, you may not *feel* you need love at all, even when you do. Also, while hunger and thirst lessen or disappear when you have had food or drink, love does not disappear when you are with your beloved. It may grow, which means that love is not sated as appetites are.

Finally, it is possible to say that love tells you something about yourself in relation to the world. To be in love informs you that your beloved is beautiful, say. It seems to you as much a fact about the world as that the earth is damp, the plate hot.

What does this all add up to? It helps us be clearer about what the experience of love is.

Consider again the idea that love is a feeling. It is true that it may be associated with feelings of agitation or bodily sensations from time to time. A lover may feel fear or anger and that may produce physiological reactions that can be measured, perhaps by a brain scanner or heart monitor. But love may also produce feelings of pride or compassion, and so a swelling or softening of the heart. These are feelings that are not empirically detectable.

The analysis suggested that behaviour is a better measure of love: sometimes, perhaps, but not always. A mother may spend a lot of time with the child she loves. Then, the child grows up and leaves home. Her love will not lessen, though now she is only with her child for a few days each year. Her behaviour has changed. Her love remains.

It seems that it is the *attitude* that she has towards her adult child that counts. The person is special to her. She has a loving stance towards him or her regardless of what she is thinking or feeling or doing. The love remains as she hangs her coat up in the office or steps off the treadmill at the gym. Even if her child dies, so that she never sees him or her again, the loving attitude is likely to remain. Once she has grieved, her subsequent behaviour may never reveal the love caught up in her loss. It still makes sense to say that she loves her child.

Love, then, is above all known in the way in which someone or something matters to you. Its shifting feelings are secondary expressions of the fact that this person is so important.

▶ The heart's reasons

This raises another dimension. Love has reasons that make us act out of love, as well as being a generator of desires, thoughts and feelings. John is prepared to go to the Indian restaurant rather than the Chinese takeaway, even though he dislikes the smell of curry, because he knows that Jane prefers Indian food. He makes a voluntary sacrifice for her because of his love. His longstanding care and concern for her, coupled to the capacity to hold his own desires and feelings in check, means that the decision to go to the Indian restaurant does not lead to a breakdown in their relationship. That is a relatively trivial example of the kind of sacrifice love can achieve – though, no doubt, relationships have also ended over less.

Conversely, because love is a kind of belief about the way things are in your world, it can also be subject to false beliefs. Goethe's famous novel *Die Leiden des jungen Werthers* (The Sorrows of Young Werther; 1774) describes how Werther is tortured by the glance that Charlotte apparently sends his way as she is descending from her carriage, though he cannot decide whether the look was accidental or intended. What does it mean? He indulges his passion and chooses not to test the beliefs he nurtures. Only they then turn out to be false. They are proven wrong when Charlotte marries Albert, and Werther is overwhelmed. He decides that he cannot hurt Charlotte or Albert, and so he shoots himself.

Again, it is not desires, thoughts and feelings alone that lead the sane victims of unrequited love to do

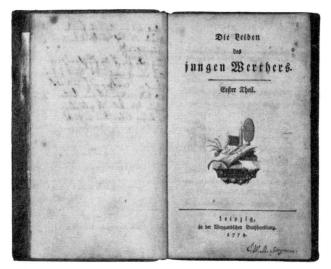

▲ The title page from the first edition of Goethe's novel of unrequited young love, *Die Leiden des jungen Werthers*.

themselves harm. Reasoning, particularly of the hot kind, is required for us to act out of love. Other admirers of Charlotte were sad, even distressed, when she married Albert, but, so far as we know, they more coolly reasoned against putting a gun to their head.

Love is a *rational* emotion, although that does not imply that lovers always understand why they feel love for one another – far from it. But they do know that they love one another and they will deliberate and do things for one another out of love. The heart has its reasons, Pascal observed.

In other words, love is not just about feelings or behaviour. It is also a commitment based upon the knowledge that the person in love gains by being in love, for all that they might be mistaken or wrong. It is fundamentally a stance towards someone or something. It is for this reason that love is not easily tested in an empirical way, because it involves far more than observable signs, and so scientific claims to have unpacked the mystery of love should be dismissed. The science of love can cast light on the subject, but a Shakespeare will always cast more because a Shakespeare can explore these inner aspects of love.

The analysis also raises the probability that animals are not capable of the same richness in love as humans. There is some overlap on the feelings and behaviour front because humans are animals, too. But, though one man may say he makes love like a rabbit, or another that he is as loyal to his partner as a swan, he is not really behaving like an animal. Sexual voraciousness and faithful monogamy are driven by human psychological imperatives unknown to rabbits or swans. Similarly, your cat may love you in a feline way, but it is unlikely to sacrifice its warm place at the hearth for you. It has to be moved to make way for you, and takes no notice of your thanks for being moved on.

Most intriguingly of all, Hacker's analysis suggests that, although our love may be hidden from the objective gaze of the scientist, it is not hidden from others whom we love, as if we have to infer that we are loved or that we love others. Love may not be as tangible as the hot plate and the damp earth. It may not readily be measurable. We can also try to hide our love, for fear of rejection or ridicule. But when we love openly – and sooner or later true love will show itself one way or another, for all that it may be unrequited – those we love know of it directly. It is not a private feeling that others only guess at from our behaviour and because they know the experience of love in themselves, too. Rather, love is shared, negatively when it is rejected. It is known between us as well as within us. We do not observe that we are in love. Together, people know it.

So, Romeo does not hope that Juliet loves him because of the way she hangs from the balcony. When he sees her longing, the thrill is that he knows it. Similarly, Juliet does not hope Romeo loves her because he is hiding in the foliage beneath. Her heart leaps because she is delighted her love is returned. Lovers love to talk about their love, it is true, and when it is going well such talk is an exploration of their mutual delight. Conversely, when lovers doubt each other, the love is already in doubt.

Hacker remarks:

> We can often see delight and rage in a person's face, joy, anguish or horror in his eyes, contempt or amusement in his smile. We can hear the love and tenderness, the grief and sorrow, the anger and contempt in a person's voice. We can observe their tears of joy or grief, cries of terror, joy or amazement, and blushes of embarrassment or shame.

> Peter Hacker, 'The conceptual framework for the investigation of emotions', *International Review of Psychiatry* 16/3 (2004), pp. 199–208 (2004)

This is how humans communicate, as permeable persons and not telegraphing machines.

In short, love is such an important affection and attitude for us humans – probably the most important – because, with love, we know we are not alone.

Love, human and divine

All of a sudden, the person who has been guided in matters of love will catch sight of something wonderfully beautiful in its nature.

The priestess Diotima,
in Plato's *Symposium*

ALL THAT MATTERS

▶ Towards the divine

Love comes in three movements. The insights of forms of knowledge as different as ancient myth and developmental psychology converge to suggest that, first, we love ourselves, although, all being well, this is but a preparation for the shock of realizing there is another in the world whom we might trust to love and be loved by, too. Love does not end there, for all that powerful myths of romantic love try to persuade us that love is fulfilled best in one other. There is another wrench to make into a third kind of love and with it comes the possibility of sharing in circles of love – family, friends, community – alongside the more subtle capacity to stand back and reflect on life and love itself.

But is there a fourth step that love affords, another dimension of existence it can open up to us? Certainly, many human beings have believed so, calling that dimension 'God', or 'the transcendent', or 'the noble truths'. The writer of the late fourteenth-century spiritual guide *The Cloud of Unknowing* talked of a 'dart of longing love' that can penetrate these clouds of our unknowing. Others have tried to live lives of compassion that bring enlightenment. So what sense can be made of such claims today?

A middle-aged man was reflecting on his life. He was suffering from a midlife crisis and was wondering how he had got to this point, when his mind reached back earlier, to his youth. He had then known a friend, a very close friend, a relationship that seemed, at the time, to capture the very best of life. It was love in all its fullness, an experience of life and connection that drew him out of himself and into the riches of the world. However, the relationship had ended tragically and badly. The friend had become ill. One night, while sitting at the sickbed, the two had argued. They parted, angry. Then, overnight, the friend took a turn for the worse. He died.

The man was heartbroken. Full of remorse, he could not bear to stay in the town he had so enjoyed with his friend. Every street and corner reminded him of the joy they had shared, joy that would be had no more. He shook the dust from his feet and tried to mourn his loss. It took 11 years. What a fool I was, he mused, to love someone as if they were a god – as if they would never die and leave me. He came close to giving up on friendship altogether, the great flowering of human love. The dependency it nurtured was too risky; the possibility of further losses too fearful.

The man in question was Augustine of Hippo, the great writer of the early Christian church. His *Confessions* contains the moving story of his youthful love. It also describes how he came to befriend others again.

In time, Augustine became persuaded that mature love creates an openness that reaches not just for others, or for life, but for nothing less than the infinite. Because they love, human beings are the creatures for whom their own existence is too small. We long for more out of life, always more. This can be found, in part, in the love of friends and the love of family, the love of science, the arts. However, truly to give yourself to these people and things carries the peril that they themselves will only awaken a deeper longing in you, one that may never be satisfied. The scientist must reconcile themselves to the fact that they will never understand it all. They must be able to tolerate the mystery their explorations unfold more than any results. The artist must be content with what is good enough, for no work of art can be called perfect – bar possibly a handful from the greatest: Leonardo's *Mona Lisa*, Bach's Brandenberg Concertos, Shakespeare's *King Lear*. And even then, there will always be debate. The *Mona Lisa* only became truly celebrated after it was stolen in 1911.

Plato realized this, too. In works like the *Symposium* and the *Phaedrus*, he provides a vivid description of the way that love works. It has the remarkable quality of revealing an experience of life that far transcends the first taste of love that awoke us to its allure. By committing to live a life in pursuit of love, Plato says, life will become far more for us than we might imagine. Love carries within itself a tremendous transformative potential. The individual who loves enough – be it as a friend, a parent, a scientific or artistic explorer – is changed as they love. Love itself seems to overcome inherent limitations, often to a surprising degree. When that change goes well, people find their capacity for loving expanding, too. They sense more and more of life.

Love and the promise of beauty

Love works in two ways, according to Irving Singer, a contemporary philosopher of love in debate with Plato. First, there is appraisal, which he describes as 'the ability to discover value, in oneself or in other people'. Then there is also bestowal, 'a way of creating value, not the same kind of value as in appraisal, but a new kind of value'. You might say that appraisal gets a relationship going because of what it discovers in another and that bestowal allows the relationship to deepen because it creates new value, not present before, that arises out of the relationship itself.

Plato would have agreed. He argued that love moves us because of the magnetic force known as beauty: the beauty we discern in our beloved is love's 'promise of happiness' should we manage to make a life together. It works in two ways. First, our appraisal of the beauty draws us to them or it, although what Plato also noticed is that at this stage we do not know precisely what we will find should we get there. This is partly because beauty awakens us from afar: its task is to draw us towards who or what is not yet known. (To put it more colloquially: a common piece of advice would be to get to know someone you have fallen in love with before making any big decisions – beauty can be skin deep and so fool us.)

But there is a more radical aspect to beauty's promise, too, because love itself creates a new future out of the relationship as it unfolds. It is not just that the beloved is at first a stranger to us. Something new happens when lovers get together. (Hence lovers quite naturally make promises to stay with one another – it is a way of saying: we do not know where love will lead.)

To put it another way, we bet on love when we respond to beauty, a bet that is 'a stab at the future' as the philosopher Alexander Nehamas puts it. This insight, Nehamas argues, is Plato's most startling: love is creative, working reflexively in the fit and friction of the relationship that is uniquely the lovers' own. 'What is mine is thine, and thine is mine', as the old phrase has it, not only because they will now share what they had separately before but because something comes into being that is forged within and belongs to their relationship. (Hence, divorce always jars, even when the love has died, because the former lovers must undo at least some of the good they together created.)

▶ Exponential love

Plato stressed that love is a tricky path to follow, one of great toil, likely setbacks, and possible failure. Human beings find themselves in something of a bind when it comes to love because the love that spontaneously arises within the individual is inevitably limited and flawed for the reason that human beings are limited and flawed creatures. We are always, in a way, failures in love.

It is a truth that chimes with developmental psychology. There are the anxious experiences that must be borne for the infant to transcend their narcissism and grant that mother has interests other than itself. These will probably not easily be remembered in adulthood, unless the individual has a crisis or braves some therapy. What most will recall is the second watershed, the first time they fell in love. The writer Richard Holloway describes this as both a troubling and an entertaining rite of passage, in his

▲ Dante Gabriel Rossetti, *Beata Beatrix*, oil on canvas, 1864–70, Tate, London. The Pre-Raphaelite artist Dante Gabriel Rossetti fell for Elizabeth Siddal, the original 'stunner'. Here she is painted as his mystical muse, suggesting the link between physical and spiritual love explored by Plato. (See, too Appendix II: Making love, body and soul: Plato on love).

memoir *Leaving Alexandria*. As a young man, he fell for a woman who was helping with the harvest on the farm where he was employed one summer holiday. She was a little older than him, and the sight of her was irresistible as the day heated up and she peeled off layer after tantalizing layer of clothing. The shape of her breasts against cotton was too much. 'I sat there, stunned,' he writes. 'And I saw what my life would be like. An endless struggle with the flesh' (*Leaving Alexandria*, p. 83).

The sense of struggle described by Holloway may be the first remembered intimation of the difficult journey that love would have the individual undertake, though it is a struggle not without hope, Plato would add. If courageous and capable, the individual is likely to undergo a transformation in which the first yearnings for another human body subtly shift and begin to speak to them of a deeper desire.

A common adult manifestation of this movement is the perhaps surprising wish to have children with a person to whom you are attracted. Children, Plato explains, are a product of love's spiritual desire for more from life. Much as Solovyov argued, sexual congress in human beings stirs up a longing that teenage lovers would never have dreamed of – a desire to overcome their egoism, felt as a longing to have and hold a new life sprung from their love.

Children can prove to be a great satisfaction. But they have a tendency to have a life of their own and routinely disrupt the hopes and longings of parents. Hence it is said that a child needs to be able to forge a life of its own, free of the shadows of parental desire. So, individuals strive for other ways of embracing more from life, too, of transcending the boundaries of their own limited existence. There are the sciences and arts, friends and work, wealth and fame. Though, again, you do not have to look too hard to feel that they are likely to offer only fragile satisfaction as well. This was Augustine's harrowing experience.

There is an element in some of these activities that can mitigate the risk to a degree – that is, when they contribute to the common good. Plato suspected that this is why people seek to make contributions to the societies in which they live. That can take many forms. Individuals become artists not only for reasons of self-expression but to make public works. Engaging in research and science not only scratches a personal itch that wants to know but contributes to the accumulation of knowledge that links the individual to wider concerns. Others may devote their loves to upholding justice, caring for others, or laying down their life for their country.

Another aspect of love that builds in a degree of resilience is creativity. Plato points out that the love of friends, wealth or discovery may be possessive – as in, this is *my* friend', *my* money', *my* insight'. But creativity may also take on a different tone, not possessive but generative. Possessive energies are transformed from being self-serving to being collaborative.

You can tell because when individuals collaborate on some project that they love, or when their collaboration is a commitment to each other born of love, the results are exponential. What they give birth to is more than either alone could have conceived. The beautiful ideas of one combine with those of another and a third thing is born. The lovers will themselves be changed by this process, as parents are when they have children. They will love something new that they could not have anticipated before their work of love began and it will take them out of themselves.

▶ The final goal of loving?

We are a long way from the youthful desire for another body. Such is the transformative potential of love. But are we any closer to discerning the possibility of a fourth shift, an awakening to the transcendent? Plato and Augustine believed so, because they made an observation something like this.

What links the later creative activities with the first romantic urge and the demands of infant love is that they promise a kind of reversal. It is not we who must cling to love out of an act of desperation, but, rather, to mature in love is to discover that love is already flowing through us, has in a sense already *made* us. The young infant did not know Mother was there, though she was. Later, it did not know that Mother was supported by the love of others, though that is revealed when the child awakens to the reality of a third.

A creative life is like that, too. It is always already born of the passion of others, always already 'standing on the shoulders of giants'. And Owen Barfield (in 'The harp and the camera') offers an analogy that extends the insight to life itself. He suggests that to be human is to be like an Aeolian harp. These musical instruments consist of a wooden box and sounding board, over which strings are stretched across a bridge. They look a little like a violin without the neck. Also, they are not played by a bow, as the violin is, but rather by the wind. Aeolian harps are placed in openings across which the wind may blow, perhaps at a window: Aeolus is the god of the wind. As the air current sweeps across the strings, so the music from the harp is heard shifting and evolving, rising and falling. We are the harp, and the wind is the love required to make the music. We have a creative part to play in the harmonies that emerge, though without the movement of pre-existing love there could only be silence.

Still, the fragility persists. Love is always a scary force. In taking us out of ourselves, placing our lives in the love of others, it places our wellbeing in their hands, too. When things go well, this fires our creativity, our capacity to give, our passion for life. When we are let down or betrayed, love generates rage, envy, desolation, the desire for destruction. You are far more likely to be murdered by someone you love than by an outsider. It is friends who can hurt you the most, not strangers.

For Augustine, though, who was very influenced by Plato's ideas, there is a way out of this terrible ambivalence. He found faith in the then new religion, Christianity. It taught him not to strive for and cling to what he thought he desired or only to turn to the love of others. It alerted him to a love that was closer to him than he was to himself and which could, at the last, always be relied upon. The sufferings of life did not cease: he was still called to love. Only now there was the promise that the hurt would be redeemed. He discovered that love's process of self-renunciation – which we have described as modes one, two and three – opened him up to a fourth dimension he had not thought possible, a sense of divine love that unfailingly underpinned it all because it created it all.

It seemed as if a final barrier had dissolved. The most basic truth in life is not that we yearn for more when clumsily we love, though we do, but that the constant, unclouded love of God yearns for us. The revelation is summed up in the formula: God is love.

Parallel intuitions can be found in other world religions. In the Upanishads, the reversal comes about inasmuch as the devotee becomes free from desire. I take this to mean that the individual must journey first into their desire in order to understand its pain and complications. This 'purification of the heart' gradually leads to a place on the other side of love, as it were, when the flawed varieties of human love have been relocated in the divine – which for believers is the source of love anyway. The difference is that the enlightened individual now sees so clearly. 'When all the desires that dwell in the heart fall away, then the mortal becomes immortal and here attains Brahman,' the holy book says.

The psychotherapist Arthur Deikman examines this final aspect of love in his book *The Observing Self*. It includes a brilliant Jewish tale that also conveys how the transformation of desire works:

> A famous traveling maggid was once preaching in a city, when word came that the rabbi of Lublin had arrived. And immediately all the maggid's audience left to greet the zaddik. The preacher found himself

quite alone. He waited for a little while and then he too saw the seer's table heaped with the 'ransom-money' which the petitioners and other visitors had brought him. The maggid asked: 'How is this possible! I have been preaching here for days and have gotten nothing, while all this came your way in a single hour!' Rabbi Yitzhak replied: 'It is probably because each awakens in the hearts of men what he cherishes in his own heart: I, the hatred of money, and you the love of it.'

A.J. Deikman, *The Observing Self: Mysticism and Psychotherapy* (Boston: Beacon Press, 1982), p. 81

Such insights are the opposite of the implicit assumptions we lived by when we were born into the world and struggled to grab and possess life, in the desperate need to survive. The truth we might eventually come to is that love's desire is most deeply satisfied by letting go, by allowing, by receiving. It is not about trying to control life. That is a necessary strategy for a time, in order that we might make something of ourselves as human beings. We all do it. Augustine did, too. He tried to master philosophy and theology, as much as he had tried to hold on to his friend – and also to his lovers: recall that one of Augustine's most-cited remarks is, 'Lord, make me chaste but not yet.'

Now, though, a different kind of presence was coming through. It was the most lovely of all. 'What do I love when I love my God?' he asks at the end of his *Confessions*. Is it the glories of creation, the intensity of existence, the wonder of the heavens, the silence of eternity? 'I asked these questions simply by gazing at these things,' he continues, 'and their beauty was all the answer they gave.' This is a love that does not seek to possess, or even to create, but to contemplate.

The capacity for friendship returned when Augustine understood that in friendship he could discern the ultimate source of human satisfaction to which life had been leading him. It is the only final response to the natural desire for more. Hence, another of his oft-cited remarks: 'Our hearts are restless until they rest in you.' It is an extension of the observation that love thrives best when we do not gaze into each other's eyes but turn together towards life. The promise is a kind of love that engages not just life, but the ground of being itself. The nineteenth-century philosopher Søren Kierkegaard caught the dynamic well when he wrote:

> *Worldly wisdom thinks that love is a relationship between man and man. Christianity teaches that love is a relationship between: man–God–man, that is, that God is the middle term. However beautiful the love relationship has been between two or more people, however complete all their enjoyment and all their bliss in mutual devotion and affection have been for them, even if all men have praised their relationship – if God and the relationship to God have been left out, then, Christianly understood, this has not been love but a mutual and enchanting illusion of love.*

Søren Kierkegaard, *Works of Love: Some Christian Reflections in the Form of Discourses* (London: Collins, 1962), pp. 112–13

It seems to me that what has been learned of love from developmental psychology, as well as what has been the longstanding wisdom of the ages, points in this divine direction. Ultimately, love is not from us. It made and makes us. Human love is the experience that inevitably oscillates between poles of possessing and releasing, struggle and rest, surface and depth, body and soul, pain and pleasure, terrestrial and celestial. And yet, without the higher poles, it may be mistaken for being defined by the possessing, struggle, surface, body and pain.

The divine element is, of course, the tricky element in a secular age. The desire to invest in family and friends, in work and creativity, is straightforward to accept – if much, much harder to pull off in life. That love might lead us on an erotic quest towards God may feel like a step too far.

Perhaps family and friends, work and the like are enough. Maybe there is nothing more in life than life and so it is futile to seek the divine. Spiritual love is deluded love. However, I suspect that this is a possibility that cannot be decided upon by reason or psychology, by myth or evidence alone. Ultimately, it can only be answered by the ever-expansive journey into life called love. If there is a way back to God, only love will reveal it to us.

This 100 ideas section gives ways you can explore the subject in more depth. It's much more than just the usual reading list.

100 IDEAS

Ten ancient texts

1   **The Bible.** The story of the ancient Hebrew people's struggle to trust the love of God, and the early Christian people's discovery that the love of God is sacrificial. Try the Song of Solomon and Isaiah, chapter 40 to the end.

2   **The Kama Sutra.** The ancient Indian text that links love human and divine.

3   **Sappho, fragments of poems.** The ancient Greek poet changed writing about love, and its pains and passions, for ever.

4   **Plato, *Symposium*.** Probably the most influential work on love of all time, containing Aristophanes' creation myth and Socrates' ladder of love.

5 **Plato, *Phaedrus.*** Almost as important as the *Symposium*, especially for its exploration of the link between erotic love and friendship.

6 **Aristotle, *Nicomachean Ethics.*** Particularly good on friendship – see, especially, Books XIII and IX.

7 **Catullus, erotic poems.** Sets the standard for bawdiness and the tragic exploration of human love.

8 **Augustine, *Confessions.*** In which Augustine describes how he discovered that God is closer to him than he is to himself.

9 **Rumi, *Masnarvi.*** The Sufi poet's exploration of the orientation required to appreciate the mystery of divine love.

10 **Anonymous, *The Cloud of Unknowing.*** The medieval spiritual classic that describes knowing God as entering a cloud of forgetting, pierced by a dart of longing love.

Ten modern philosophies of love

11 **Jean-Jacques Rousseau, *Julie, or the New Heloise.*** A massive bestseller in its day, it explores many themes associated with love such as authenticity won through passion.

12 **Søren Kierkegaard, *Works of Love.*** The radical Christian philosopher's exploration of love's high demands.

13 **Denis de Rougemont, *Love in the Western World.*** A scholarly recovery of the importance of medieval traditions of courtly love.

14 **Iris Murdoch, *The Sovereignty of Good.*** Probably the most fluent English Platonist of the twentieth century.

15 Michel Foucault, *The History of Sexuality:* Volume 1: *The Will to Knowledge.* Tracks how the practices of love have shaped our sense of self.

16 Irving Singer, *The Nature of Love*, in three volumes. The influential contemporary philosopher's this-worldly account of love.

17 Martha Nussbaum, *Love's Knowledge: Essays on Philosophy and Literature.* The title essay argues that love, and only love, can teach us certain things.

18 Roger Scruton, *Sexual Desire.* An influential, relatively recent text that draws links between sexuality and the sacred.

19 Mark Vernon, *The Meaning of Friendship.* The author's own study of the perils and promise of friendship.

20 Simon May, *Love: A History.* Arguing that our understanding of love has become distorted by being held up against the unconditional love of God.

Ten psychological reads

21 Stendhal, *Love.* Coins many brilliant metaphors for love, not least how affection crystallizes around the beloved.

22 Sigmund Freud, *Three Essays on the Theory of Sexuality.* Probably Freud's most controversial texts on love, outlining his ideas about infantile sexuality.

23 Donald Winnicott, 'Primitive Emotional Development' and other papers. The under-read British psychotherapist who described good-enough mothering and the concept of holding.

24 John Bowlby, *The Making and Breaking of Affectional Bonds.* Attachment theory described in a series of essays by the main figure in the field.

25 Daniel Stern, *The Interpersonal World of the Infant: A View from Psychoanalysis and Development Psychology.* Helpfully bridges the two worlds of therapy and behavioural studies.

26 Carol Gilligan, *In a Different Voice: Psychological Theory and Women's Development.* How women might be from Venus.

27 Darian Leader, *Why Do Women Write More Letters Than They Post?* The Lacanian psychoanalyst revels in the contradictions of love.

28 Susie Orbach, *The Impossibility of Sex.* Study of the relationships between clients and therapists told through fictional case histories; written by a feminist writer and psychotherapist.

29 Sue Gerhardt, *Why Love Matters: How Affection Shapes a Baby's Brain.* Excellent summary of the latest in brain and developmental psychology.

30 Lisa Appignanesi, *All About Love: Anatomy of An Unruly Emotion.* The popular psychotherapist knits together personal and professional insights.

Ten personal reads

31 Abelard and Heloise, *The Love Letters.* A searingly painful account of a medieval love affair.

32 Shakespeare, *Romeo and Juliet.* Not the only play in which love is a central theme, but probably the most famous. There are also, of course, the sonnets (see **43** and **44** below).

33 Gustave Flaubert, *Madame Bovary.* The classic story of love that becomes obsessive.

34 Jane Austen, *Pride and Prejudice.* This and all her other novels trace the ups and downs of falling in love.

35 Leo Tolstoy, *Anna Karenina.* A profound moral examination of love by one of the great Russian writers and called by some the greatest novel.

36 Marcel Proust, *In Search of Lost Time.* The great French novelist is pessimistic about romantic love but understands its thrills.

37 Roland Barthes, *A Lover's Discourse.* Brilliant and aphoristic on the experience of love, this manages to be both familiar and unsettling.

38 Edmund White, *A Boy's Own Story.* Autobiographical and ground-breaking rendition of the agonies and pleasures of growing up gay.

39 Helen Fielding, *Bridget Jones's Diary.* Entertaining account of urban singledom coming up against married life.

40 Ian McEwan, *On Chesil Beach.* A desperate tale of how fears about sex and marriage can change lives for ever.

Ten poems

41 'Love shock my heart / Like the wind on the mountain' by Sappho.

42 'The Flea' by John Donne, which makes the insect into a romantic symbol.

43 Sonnet 116 by William Shakespeare, the one about love being unchanging.

44 Sonnet 130 by William Shakespeare, which is fragrant with feeling.

45 'Wild Nights' by Emily Dickinson, which takes the breath away with its passion.

46 'And What Is Love?' by John Keats, a wry look from the Romantic poet.

47 'A Red, Red Rose' by Robert Burns. His love is like the quintessential romantic flower.

48 'Body, Remember' by C.P. Cavafy, which evokes the carnal experience of love.

49 'How Do I Love Thee?' by Elizabeth Barrett Browning, the one that counts the ways.

50 'Rapture' by Carol Ann Duffy, which remakes Sappho's lines for the twenty-first century.

Ten phrases and sayings

51 'Cupid's dart.' A figure of speech derived from the imagery of the Cupid, the Roman god of love, often pictured with a bow and arrow.

52 'To love and be wise is scarcely allowed to God.' Latin proverb coined by Publilius Syrus in the first century BC.

53 'Love is blind.' English proverb, late fourteenth century.

54 'The quarrel of lovers is the renewal of love.' English proverb, early sixteenth century.

55 'Love and a cough cannot be hid.' English proverb, early sixteenth century.

56 'The course of love never did run smooth.' English proverb, late sixteenth century.

57 'Love will find a way.' English proverb, early seventeenth century.

58 'Love means never having to say you're sorry.' Advertising copy for the film *Love Story* (1970).

59 'Love begets love.' English proverb, early sixteenth century.

60 'Love laughs at locksmiths.' English proverb, early nineteenth century.

Ten old quotes

61 'Many waters cannot quench love, neither can the floods drown it.' Song of Solomon 8:7

62 'Love conquers all things: let us too give in to Love.' Virgil, *Eclogues* X, line 69

63 'There is no fear in love; but perfect love casteth out fear.' 1 John 4:18

64 'And now abideth faith, hope, love, these three; but the greatest of these is love.' 1 Corinthians 13:13

65 '[T]he love that moves the sun and the other stars.' Dante Alighieri, *Paradise*, Canto XXXIII, lines 142–5

66 'Who ever loved that loved not at first sight?' Christopher Marlowe, *Hero and Leander*

67 'Love is like linen often changed, the sweeter.' Phineas Fletcher

68 'Love is not love / Which alters when it alteration finds.' William Shakespeare, Sonnet 116, lines 2–3

69 'Love is the fart / Of every heart.' John Suckling

70 'There is no disguise which can hide love for long where it exists, or feign it where it does not.' Duc de la Rochefoucauld, *Maxims*, 70

Ten modern quotes

71 'The magic of first love is our ignorance that it can ever end.' Benjamin Disraeli

72 'If you could see my legs when I take my boots off, you'd form some idea of what unrequited affection is.' Charles Dickens

73 'Tis better to have loved and lost/Than never to have loved at all.' Alfred, Lord Tennyson

74 'The love that lasts longest is the love that is never returned.' Somerset Maugham

75 'Yet each man kills the thing he loves.' Oscar Wilde

76 'The fate of love is that it always seems too little or too much.' Amelia E. Barr

77 'Experience shows us that love does not consist in gazing at each other but in looking together in the same direction.' Antoine de Saint-Exupéry

78 'If I can't love Hitler, I can't love at all.' A.J. Muste

79 'What will survive of us is love.' Philip Larkin

80 'All you need is love.' John Lennon and Paul McCartney

Ten fictional narcissists

81 Lucifer, in *Paradise Lost*, who, according to Milton, is thrust into hell, where there is 'neither joy, nor love, but fierce desire'.

82 Dorian Gray, in Oscar Wilde's *The Picture of Dorian Gray*, who sells his soul to preserve his handsome visage for ever, while his portrait ages and grows ugly.

83 Norma Desmond, in the film *Sunset Boulevard*, played by Gloria Swanson, exposing what one reviewer called the Hollywood 'narcissistic hellhole'.

84 The character in Frank Sinatra's song, 'My Way', who comforts himself in the face of impending death with the knowledge that he did it his way.

85 Jean-Paul Sartre's existential heroes have been called narcissistic because they attempt to save their sense of self by being detached and aloof.

86 Iron Man, from the Marvel comic series, who as a vain superhero is actually trapped inside his metal suit, strangely detached from the world.

87 Patrick Bateman, in *American Psycho*, who has no feelings for his fellow human beings and whose real life blurs with his fantasy life.

88 Zaphod Beeblebrox, in *The Hitchhiker's Guide to the Galaxy*, who is wildly insensitive to those around him and 'relaxes' by becoming more and more tense.

89 Suzanne Stone-Maretto, in the film *To Die For*, played by Nicole Kidman, who would murder her husband to appear on television.

90 Narcissa Malfoy, in the Harry Potter novels, who is obsessed with blood purity and obscenely devoted to her son, sending him cakes every day.

Ten artworks

91 *Venus and Mars* by Sandro Botticelli. The amorous god and goddess look exhausted, if satisfied.

92 *Venus with Mercury and Cupid (The School of Love)* by Correggio. A tender representation of familial love.

Appendix II: Making love, body and soul: Plato on love

Readers will realize that my feelings about love, such as they are, are frequently guided and shaped by Plato. Even when I have drawn on Freud and his critical successors, Plato is never far away: Freud himself referred to the ancient Greek philosopher, and pupil of Socrates, as the 'divine Plato', indicating what an inspiration he is.

In short, Plato is the greatest thinker on love the West has ever known, though to say as much is not so controversial. What is more unusual today, among philosophers at least, is to believe that what Plato wrote, in many respects, stands the test of time.

In the second half of the twentieth century a number of weighty criticisms were levelled against Plato and they almost wrecked his reputation. I suspect the high tide of anti-Platonic feeling is passing. But to do my little bit to keep up the momentum, I would like to consider the major charge against him put by the scholar Gregory Vlastos. We can learn something more about love at the same time.

Vlastos wrote a paper, now famous among students of ancient Greek philosophy, entitled 'The individual as object of love in Plato' (included in his *Platonic Studies*

(Princeton: Princeton University Press, 1973)). In it, he argued that Plato's conception of love looks glorious but is, in fact, abhorrent. It is abusive. Plato charts a view of love that is awakened by being drawn to other people, by falling in love. However, he then goes on, Vlastos believed, to advocate a path that gradually discards human loves and lovers in favour of presumed higher goals of love that come into view. In other words, Plato's philosophy of love advocates that you should use others to stir love in you before dumping them in favour of what he believes the human soul really yearns for – that which is most beautiful, good and true; in a word, God. This treats human beings not as ends in themselves, but as means to other more lofty ends and goals. It is an inhuman philosophy of love and one that is deeply offensive to modern sensibilities, going against basic ethical principles.

Thankfully, a newer generation of scholars, not least Alexander Nehamas, have shown that this is a serious misreading. (Two books by Nehamas are good reads – *The Art of Living: Socratic Reflections from Plato to Foucault* and *Only a Promise of Happiness: The Place of Beauty in a World of Art* – though, if you want to get to the nub of his argument about Plato, he gave a brilliant lecture on how to read Plato, entitled 'Only in the contemplation of beauty is human life worth living', published in the *European Journal of Philosophy* 15/1 (2007), pp. 1–18, which at the time of writing was available free online.)

Think of it this way. You may be the kind of person who admires red hair, to the extent that you feel the greatest beauties in the world are individuals with flaming locks. You are in good company. As we noted in Chapter 9, no less an artist than Dante Gabriel Rossetti would agree. When he met Elizabeth Siddal, whose red hair flowed along her shoulders, he felt 'his destiny was defined'. It has been said that his portraits of her turned Siddal into the first supermodel and Rossetti invented the word 'stunner' to describe her. The art critic John Ruskin agreed that Siddal's 'red gold hair, ethereal colouring, large limpid eyes [had the] look of someone in a medieval Florentine fresco'. High praise indeed.

But does that mean Rossetti loved Siddal's hair and her hair alone? Not at all. His relationship with her was complicated, not least by his affair with another woman, Fanny Cornforth. (Another of the dangers of a life devoted to love is the tendency to promiscuity.) She had a 'mass of the most lovely blonde hair – light golden or harvest yellow'. But then, when his first love, Siddal, died, Rossetti was filled with remorse. He buried her with a book of unfinished poems tucked under her head and began to paint her as Beata Beatrix, a mystical muse. He would not have done that had his love been for her hair alone. Had that been so, someone else endowed with equally luxurious flames could have simply replaced her.

Vlastos's charge is that Plato's philosophy of love implies we love individuals for something about them that is beautiful – like red hair – and we then discard them when we see things in other individuals that embody that beauty more deeply. But Rossetti's story shows that human love does not work like that, and Plato did not think it worked like that either. To love someone for a single feature alone – be it hair, eyes, ankles, physique, bust, wit, intelligence, stamina or anything else – is not love. It is a fetish. And the trouble with fetishes is that they get stuck. They do not spark the capacity to love life more deeply and broadly. And this is what Plato searched for from love and which was the test of true love for him.

It is true that Plato believed that 'higher loves' will be longer lasting than the love of human bodies. And this is only to state something known by anyone who has been in an enduring relationship. At first the body of your beloved draws you. There is a thrill in just touching. And then, in time, the physical intimacy shifts in quality. It becomes the vehicle of a deeper connection, expressive of a communication that is charged not only by body but by soul, too. When you make love, you caress with heart and mind. To put it more generally, what Plato discerned was that the love of what is good, beautiful and true will be the most profound and engaging love of all.

In a theist context, this is to say that the love of God will grip human beings to the core of their being. From that, it does not follow that you will or should discard those individuals whom you love. Rather, lovers can come to share the spiritual experience as part of their lives together. After all, what Christian, Muslim or Jew has argued that the love of God should be to the detriment of the love of their fellows? In fact, all three monotheistic faiths argue precisely the opposite: they place the love of others at the centre of the life of faith. Plato championed a version of this so-called Golden Rule, too.

In fact, it seems likely that the irreplaceable value of other human beings will be underlined, not undermined, by the gradual realization of higher loves. This is because that which is good and beautiful in someone will come to take on a deeper intensity as the eye of the soul is opened, to use Plato's phrase. With the spiritual awakening that love inspires, the beloved will look more beautiful, not less. To put it more colloquially, it might be said that such an enlightened person will 'see the best in us', that which we perhaps don't see ourselves. Further, the more someone has embraced the life of love, the more they will want more from us, not less.

This is precisely how Plato's dialogues depict Socrates in his interactions with his friends. And, for Plato, there is no higher exemplar of the life of love he commends.

Select bibliography

Appignanesi, L., *All about Love: Anatomy of an Unruly Emotion* (London: Virago, 2011)

Badiou, A., with N. Truong, *In Praise of Love* (London: Serpent's Tail, 2009)

Barfield, O., 'The harp and the camera', in *The Rediscovery of Meaning and Other Essays* (San Rafael, CA: Barfield Press, 1977), pp. 74–89

Bartels, A. and Zeki, S., 'The neural basis of romantic love', *NeuroReport* 11/7 (2000), pp. 3829–34

Britton, R., 'The missing link: parental sexuality in the Oedipus complex', in R. Britton, M. Fledman and E. O'Shaughnessy (eds), *The Oedipus Complex Today* (London: Karnac Books, 1989), p. 87

Buber, M., *I And Thou*, trans. Ronald Gregor Smith (London: Continuum, 2008)

Deikman, A.J., *The Observing Self: Mysticism and Psychotherapy* (Boston: Beacon Press, 1982)

E.M. Forster, *A Room with a View* (Mineola, NY: Dover Thrift Editions, 1995)

Greene, G., *The Power and the Glory* (London: Vintage, 2001), p. 6

Hacker, P., 'The conceptual framework for the investigation of emotions', *International Review of*

Psychiatry 16/3 (2004), pp. 199–208 (2004); available online at http://info.sjc.ox.ac.uk/scr/hacker/docs/Emotions%20-%20conceptual%20framework.pdf

Hellinger, B., *Love's Hidden Symmetries* (Phoenix: Zeig, Tucker & Co., 1998)

Holloway, R., *Leaving Alexandria: A Memoir of Faith and Doubt* (Edinburgh: Canongate Books, 2012)

Kierkegaard, S., *Works of Love: Some Christian Reflections in the Form of Discourses* (London: Collins, 1962), pp. 112–13

May, S., *Love: A History* (New Haven: Yale University Press, 2011)

Moore, T., *Care of the Soul* (London: HarperCollins, 1992), p. 72

Nehamas, A., 'Only in the contemplation of beauty is human life worth living', *European Journal of Philosophy* 15/1 (2007), pp. 1–18

Plato, *Phaedrus*, trans. Alexander Nehamas and Paul Woodruff (Indianapolis: Hackett Publishing Company, 1995), 255B

Proust, M., *In Search of Lost Time*, vol. 5, trans. C.K. Scott Moncrieff, T. Kilmartin and D.J. Enright (London: Modern Library Edition)

Roth, P., 'The depressive position', in S. Budd and R. Rusbridger (eds), *Introducing Psychoanalysis* (Hove: Routledge, 2005), p. 52

Schopenhauer, A., *The World as Will and Representation*, vol. 2 (New York: Dover Publications, 1966), pp. 533–4

Solovyov, V., *The Meaning of Love*, trans. Thomas R. Beyer and introd. Owen Barfield (Herndon, VA: Lindisfarne Press, 1985)

Tallis, R., *Aping Mankind: Neuromania, Darwinitis and the Misrepresentation of Humanity* (Durham: Acumen, 2011), p. 77

Themistius, *Orations* 24, 'An exhortation to the Nicomedians'

Tolstoy, L., 'Happy Ever After', *The Kreutzer Sonata and Other Stories*, trans. Louise and Aylmer Maude and J.D. Duff (Oxford: Oxford University Press, 2009), pp. 3–84

Vlastos, G., 'The individual as object of love in Plato', in *Platonic Studies* (Princeton: Princeton University Press, 1973)

Waddell, M., *Inside Lives: Psychoanalysis and the Growth of the Personality* (New York: Routledge, 1998)

Index

ALL THAT MATTERS: LOVE

Acknowledgements

Love is one of those subjects that fundamentally one learns about in a basic, bodily way from those with whom one is connected by love. In addition, I would like to thank Ziyad Marar, Robert Roland Smith and Simon May who read versions of the manuscript and made very helpful suggestions. I much appreciate the time and effort put into the book by folk at Hodder Education and also by editor, Robert Anderson. Heartfelt thanks, too, to Colin Campbell and Margaret Sheehan for many wise hours.

Picture credits

The author and publisher would like to give their thanks for permission to use the following images:

Cupid and Psyche by Jacques-Louis David. © Bettmann/ CORBIS

Portrait of Princess Louise Augusta of Denmark as a Child by Helfrich Peter Sturz. © Danish Royal Collections, Rosenborg Castle

Illustration by John Tenniel from *Alice's Adventures in Wonderland* by Lewis Carroll, 1865. © Heritage Images/ Corbis

his birth, he was recognized as a child of outstanding beauty. Onlookers gasped as he lay in the cradle. He appeared so perfect that some feared he might not live. It was as if such faultlessness could not survive the ravages of the world. As a psychologist might say today, the young infant was vulnerable. His beauty secured the narcissistic attention he needed.

The myth continues with strange words from the prophet Tiresias. When asked, he thought that the child would live so long as he did not come to know himself. It struck his auditors as an odd reflection. Knowing yourself seems a good dictum in life. But Tiresias was a seer. He could see what would happen if a child catches a glimpse of its magical good looks.

Narcissus grew up and his beauty deepened. It resonated from deep within his body. Over his shoulder you could see a line of devastated individuals who had fallen in love with him as he walked into, and then out of, their lives. The crowds would part like the sea as he strode through the marketplace. As for himself, he hardly noticed those who were infatuated. He developed an air of aloofness and hard pride. It was as if others did not really exist for him, as if he was the only person in the world. Those who saw this attitude were chilled by it. They did not come near him, for all that another part of them longed to hold him, too.

One day Narcissus was hunting in the woods and was spotted by Echo, another nymph. She had been punished for trickery by Hera, the wife of Zeus. Her own voice had been taken away and now all she could do was repeat the words of others. She was beautiful, too, though the habit of replicating and recapping the words of others – and never uttering anything for herself – meant that she had gained a reputation as a gossip.

In the woods, Echo caught sight of Narcissus and, of course, instantly fell overwhelmingly in love. She followed him through the grove like a hungry lioness tracking a gazelle. She longed to call out to him but words failed her. She could only wait.

Narcissus had set off with a group of youthful peers, though, as often happened, he had wandered off on his own, only now noticing that they were no longer with him. 'Where are you?' he shouted. 'I'm here,' he continued, narcissistically assuming that they would come running to him, as his mother always had.

Echo seized her chance. 'I'm here,' she called. 'I'm here... I'm here... I'm here...'

Narcissus looked up, affronted. This was an unexpected voice, and what was more, it seemed to be beckoning *him* to join *it*, not the other way round. 'Come over here,' he retorted. And Echo repeated, 'Come over here... over here... over here.'

Now irritated, Narcissus moved towards the voice. Echo emerged from the undergrowth to meet him, her heart pounding, her eyes streaming tears. It was love, though to Narcissus the emotion made her look monstrous. In fact, that was how people tended to appear to him.

He thought humanity, on the whole, repugnant. To be touched by others would be to be soiled by them. The prospect made his skin crawl. So he stepped back and immediately Echo saw that her love was unrequited. Her longing for him could now only be an agony for her to bear. She slipped back into the woods, as Narcissus turned away. There, she tended her hurt and faded and died, like an echo absorbed by the mountains.

Giving up on his companions, Narcissus made his way through the woods until he stumbled across a clear pool. The water was still and cool – just what he needed to freshen up from his journey. Not that Narcissus was grateful. He was used to the world providing for his needs.

He approached the low bank. He knelt down in the fresh grass. He lowered his head so as to drink… and caught sight of a great beauty. At last, staring back at him out of the water was someone whom he could love. Narcissus' skin did not crawl. This man's eyes were not red, his demeanour was calm. Narcissus was in love. He lay transfixed.

Now, though, it was his turn to be tortured. The face would come close to him, as he came closer to it, only to disappear the moment their lips might have touched. Similarly, if he reached out to hold the statuesque body, the lovely form dissolved in ripples of water. He did not understand that he saw his own reflection. Narcissus had no conception of the difference between subject and object. The world was undifferentiated, one. As

Ted Hughes brilliantly translates this crucial section of the story in Ovid's telling in the *Metamorphoses*: 'Not recognizing himself / He wanted only himself' (*Tales from Ovid* (Faber & Faber, 1979), p. 79).

Narcissus stayed at the water's edge, not eating, not sleeping. He called out to the trees that they should bear witness to his love. 'It is perfect,' he told them. 'He loves me, as I love him, and yet we are unable to be close.' He became angry with the image, charging it with teasing him, dodging him, tormenting him.

Then, something shifted inside. A new awareness dawned. *He* was the image. He realized that it was he who was mirrored in the stillness of the pool. He was in love with himself. He was what he desired. Only, paradoxically, that meant he could not reach out to his beloved. Narcissism left him stranded, alone, desperate. Worse, the habit was too strong. That is the agony of narcissism, not that the narcissistic person loves themselves, but that they cannot.

Narcissus longed for death as the only escape. And so he died. The story ends, when later his companions came to bury the body. What they found was a yellow-and-white flower in the place where he had lain: a narcissus.